On the Phone with Ray

Real conversations with real telemarketers

A series of actual phone conversations with Ray

Copyright ©2018 Raymond Glenn

All rights reserved. No part of this book may be reproduced or transmitted in any form or by any means, electronic or mechanical, including photocopying, recording or by any information storage and retrieval system, without the written permission of the Publisher or Author, except where permitted by law.

The Author has made a sincere effort to present the facts and circumstances related to his phone conversations, though due to the almost twenty years in progress, some of the names of the people he had been in contact with may be inaccurate. He would like to apologize for any such errors: "If you were the person I was talking to and I got your name wrong, I am truly sorry."

ISBN: 978-1-71917-271-4

Acknowledgements

[before]

I went too tank my god freind Westley Turner fur his help on putting his book unto producing. He's intention two D-tale were assume. His crazy. about English language, understand and know it. He erudited my storyes unt maked accessory changes to made thin flower correct. Westley was truely unmazing.

The conversions were reel. The furst names is correct as I collect them. The list names are phoney. The phone num for the IRS Scam is reel. Give then a call if you won't.

[after]

I want to thank my good friend Westley Turner for his help in putting this book into production. His attention to detail was awesome. His understanding and knowledge of the English language is crazy. He edited my stories and made the necessary changes to make them flow correctly. Westley is truly amazing.

The conversations were real. The first names are correct as I remember them. The last names are made up, though the phone number for the IRS Scam is a real number—give them a call if you want.

[see what I have to put up with? ed.]

Credits

Photographs of Ray by Thomas "Teejay" Joel

Book cover designed by IAMTEEJAY

                    IAMTEEJAY
          CEO Thomas "Teejay" Joel

Teejay has 24 years of website and graphic design experience and has designed covers for over 20 authors and 30 titles. He is based in Los Angeles, San Francisco, and Sacramento.

            https://www.iamteejay.com

Note from Teejay:
I play a lot of poker with Ray, and I lost an all-in bet (full house, Queens over nines, to a Jack high straight flush), so I chose to design his book cover.

Preface

The basis for this book stems from my story telling. I would constantly tell friends and acquaintances about antics that I had pulled on different people. Whether I was in a grocery store placing a watermelon in someone else's shopping cart or being that guy that happens to walk by when everyone in a group is saying goodbye and jumping in to get the good bye hugs, too, I was always in the middle of the action.

So, like everyone, I would receive telemarketing calls, and I used to just hang up on them, but all that changed when I started getting phone calls for my wife about past due bills that she had acquired before we were married. They wouldn't leave us alone, so one time I decided to tell them she was dead. That didn't work, so instead I started talking to them. Telling them stories. Keeping them on the line. I had heard that they were not supposed to hang up, but I wasn't sure, so I wanted to test it out. I would talk and talk and talk. They listened. All of them. It got to the point that every telemarketer that called me was going to spend some time getting to know me. They were convinced that they had something I needed or would need in some way, but I played dumb, confused, and lost. Over fifteen years I have talked to so many people, I can't keep track of them all.

As I told the stories about my phone calls, my friends would tell me I should write them down. So I did.

Now, I will admit that I'm not a writer—I'm a story teller, and these are some of my stories.

Contents

1. 200 Apples 1
2. Lower Interest Rates 11
3. Magazines 17
4. EarthLink 23
5. Dell 29
6. Sorry you died...again 35
7. The Loan 39
8. Health Insurance 45
9. The IRS 51
10. A New Credit Card 57
11. Solar Power 61
12. The PACE Program 65
13. Police Officers Association 69
14. ASPCA 75
15. National Auto Insurance 79
16. World Wide Vacations 85
17. Federal Grant Program 91
18. US Mortuary 99

200 Apples

Sitting in a lawn chair with my bare feet in the sand, I stared out at my kids playing in the lake, and my cell phone rings. I answer, "Hello."

A man tells me that my computer is running slow. I am intrigued that this man can tell that my computer is running slow when I'm not even home, so I ask, "Who is this?"

"This is Carl. I work for Comp-U-Tek, and we can tell that your computer is running very slow."

"Really? I thought there was something wrong."

"Yes. It is probably infected," he says.

"No! I've heard that that can happen. What do I do?"

"Not to worry. We can help you," he assures me.

"Ok, what do I do?"

"First we need you to get onto the internet."

A Frisbee suddenly whizzes by and knocks over my ice tea. I yell at the kids, "Watch it!!"

Carl continues, "Yes, you can watch it."

"Watch what?"

"You can watch the internet."

"I don't have the internet."

"You cannot go online?"

"No," I say and stand up, brushing the ice out of my lap.

"That's why you are running so slowly."

"Seriously, I knew there was a problem. I just didn't know why it took so long to do stuff."

"Yep. That is the problem. We can see that you are not connected."

"So, what do I do now?" I walk over to the picnic table and pour another cup of ice tea. I grab some chips before I return to my chair.

"We need to get you connected to the internet."

"I'm in. What do I do?"

"Who is the local provider?"

"Well there are quite a few. There is a soup kitchen downtown that provides meals. The Mission on 4th street provides meals as well. A few of the churches provide overnight sleeping...."

"No, who is your *Internet* provider?"

"Oh. Comcast I think."

"Can you get Comcast?"

"Well I need to if my computer is infected, right?"

"Yes that is correct. We cannot fix your computer until you are connected to the Internet."

"Ok. Got it."

"When can you get connected?"

"Well it's Sunday, and I don't think they are working today, but I'll call them right now and see what I can do. Can you call me back in an hour?"

"That is not a problem. I will call you in one hour."

"Thanks, Carl. You are so helpful. Don't forget about me."

"I will call you back. I promise."

"Ok, bye-bye." I hung up, got up out of my lawn chair to refill my tea, and jumped into the lake to cool off. I received a call from Carl in almost exactly one hour.

I disguised my voice as I answer. "Hello?"

"Hello, this is Carl from Comp-U-Tek, May I speak to Ray?"

Still disguising my voice, I said, "Sure, Hold on." I pause a few moments, then ask, "Who is this again?"

"This is Carl from Comp-U-Tek. I was speaking with Ray about an hour ago."

I tried a different, higher pitched voice. "Hello?"

"Hello, this is Carl from Comp-U-Tek. Is this Ray?"

"Yes," I say, still in the high pitched voice.

"You sound different."

"Different? From what? Who is this again?"

"This is Carl from Comp-U-Tek. I was speaking with you about an hour ago...about your computer."

"Oh, I'm sorry…you want my dad. I was named after him. I'm Ray Jr. Let me go find him." I wait about a minute, then continue in my normal voice. "Hello?"

"Hello, this is Carl from Comp-U-Tek. Is this Ray?"

"No…Ha, ha Just kidding. Hi, Carl. I guess my son answered the phone. He does that a lot. What a kidder. Do you have any kids?"

"Yes, I have two boys."

"Do they play around like that?"

"No, they are 4 and 6 years old."

"Ah, young ones. I have two wonderful daughters 17 and 19…oh, and another one."

"How old is your son?"

I grinned. Now I've got *him* off topic, but I continued. "Unfortunately, he's only 17. He'll be 18 in four months, and then…" with a bit of menace in my voice, "…bye-bye…" I waited for a bit, but Carl isn't talking. "Hello?" I said.

"Yes, that kind of caught me off guard."

"What?"

"About your son."

"What about him?"

"Well the…bye-bye part was really strange."

"Why was that strange?"

"I don't know."

"That's what you say to someone when they are leaving, right?"

"True, but it was *how* you said it."

"Said what?"

"Bye-bye."

"What should I say? So long, have a good trip, see you later, catch you on the flip side, hasta la vista, chow, farewell, adios, ta-ta, au revoir, cheerio…we just say bye-bye here."

"I'm—"

I don't let him get a word in. "My son is starting Officer Candidate School in September. I am so proud of him."

"That is great."

"Thanks."

He tried to get back to his script. "Were you able to connect to the Internet?"

"Not yet. I called Comcast, but all they said was that someone could come out tomorrow between 8am and 12 pm."

"Do you want me to call you then?"

"Yes. I need my computer, and faster would be better."

"Yes it would be. I will call you at 12 tomorrow afternoon."

"That would be great. I am going to take the day off from work, so I can be here when they come."

"I will talk to you tomorrow."

"Bye-bye."

I hung up, finished my outing at the lake with my family, and headed home, anticipating Carl's call. The next day I got a call at 12:05 pm.

Using my high voice disguise, I answered, "Hello?"

"Hello, this is Carl from Comp-U-Tek, May I speak to Ray?"

Same high pitched voice. "This is Ray."

"Sorry. May I speak to Ray Senior?" Ah! He caught on.

"Hold on. He is outside with somebody. I'll go get him."

"Thank you."

"No problem, wait a minute." About two minutes later, I continued...still high pitched. "He'll be right in."

"Thank you."

I waited a bit, then asked, high pitched, "Hello?"

"Is this Ray? Senior?"

"Hasn't he picked up the phone yet?"

"No. Not yet."

"Oh, here he comes. Dad, it is someone from...Hold on. Who is this again?" I ask Carl.

"This is Carl from Comp-U-Tek."

"Dad, it's Carl from Comp-U-Tek."

I rattled the phone for a moment, then continued in my normal voice. "Hello?"

"Hello, this is Carl from Comp-U-Tek."
"Hello."
"I guess you have internet now?"
"Not yet. Allen is still working on it."
"Do you know how long it will be?"
"Allen said that it might be an hour or so."
"Why don't I call back in an hour?"
"Ok, bye-bye."

It was a little over an hour before my cell phone rang again. I answered, "Hello?"

"Hello, this is Carl from Comp-U-Tek, May I speak to Ray?"
"Hi, Carl. This is Ray."
"Well are you ready to get that computer fixed up and running faster?"
"Yes, I am."
"Well let's get started. Are you in front of your computer now?"
"I am."
"Good. What do you see?"
"A black screen."
"Is the computer on?"
"No."
"Turn on your computer."
"Ok."
"Let me know when it has started."
"Ok." I wait a bit, then say, "Ok it's on."
"Good. Do you see the key that looks like four squares?"
"I do."
"Press that key and the 'R' key at the same time."
"Ok"
"What do you see?"
"Nothing."
"What opened?"
"Nothing."
"Nothing?"

"Nothing. Nothing happened."

"Nothing?"

"Nothing."

"You don't see a box?"

"No, there is nothing there."

"What do you mean nothing?"

"There is nothing. The screen is blank."

"Hit the escape button."

"Ok."

"Now what happened?"

"Nothing."

"Nothing?"

"Nothing happened. Now I am worried. You said that I had a virus. Is this what you are talking about?"

"I am afraid so. This is bad."

"Are you kidding me?"

"No. This is very serious."

"Carl, you have to help me. I need my computer."

"Ray, we are here to help. This is an easy fix."

"I hope so. I have heard people lose everything when this happens."

"They do, but I believe that we have caught it in time."

"Good. You're like a computer doctor."

"I am."

"So, what do I need to do?"

"We are going to try a different method to fix it. Are you near a Walmart?"

"Not to close. It's about four miles away."

"Not bad. Can you go to Walmart and buy two $100.00 Apple cards?"

"I can. It may take a while. I don't have a car and need to walk up there, but I do it all the time. I takes me about an hour up and a little longer coming back because I am usually carrying bags."

"When do you think you would be able to get to Walmart?"

"It's 1:57 now, if I left in 5 minutes…I would be there at 3:09…no wait 57 plus 5 is 62 which is 1 hour and 2 minutes. 1:57 plus 1 hour and 2 minutes is 2:59. I will be there at 2:59."

"Oh—"

"Wait, I forgot the 5 minutes…so 3:04."

"Oh—"

"Wait, the 5 minutes is added to the 1:57, so 2:02 and an hour to get there. I could be there by 3:02."

"Gre—"

"No I can't there by then because it is 2:04 now, and I haven't left."

"Ray?"

"Sorry, what?"

"Why don't I call you at 7 pm?"

"I should be back by then. Perfect."

"Ok. Talk to you soon."

"Bye-bye." I hung up and sat back. I can't believe that this guy, Carl, was still talking to me, but hey, I love to talk. As expected my phone rang right about 7pm.

I pick up. "Hello?"

"Hello. This is Carl from Comp-U-Tek. Is this Ray?"

"Yes."

"You made it to Walmart?"

"I did. Man that was the hardest trip to Walmart I have ever made."

"Is everything ok?"

"I just barely got home."

"Oh my."

"And now my table is covered in apples."

"I'm sorry…what?"

"My table is covered in apples."

"I don't understand."

"My table is covered in apples. You told me to go to Walmart and buy $200 worth of apples."

"No, I said go buy two $100 Apple cards."

"You said go buy $200 worth of apples. Do you know how heavy $200 worth of apples is? I had to carry a couple of the bags about 30 yards, drop them on the sidewalk, go back the 30 yards to get more bags, and keep going. It was tough but I shuffled all those apples home. I don't understand how they are going to fix my computer virus, but, hey, you are the expert."

"I believe that you misunderstood me."

I ask angrily, "What do you mean?"

"I wanted you to buy two *cards* from Walmart. They are like credit cards. Get two $100 Apple cards."

"Wow. That would have been a lot easier to carry."

"I can see the misunderstanding."

"What I am going to do with all these apples? Can't make a pie. I don't bake."

"I'm not sure."

"I guess I could return them. Man, that's going to be difficult."

"Should I call you back?"

"Yes. Can you call me tomorrow night at 6pm?"

"I surely can."

"Ok, bye-bye." I cannot believe how patient Carl has been with me, but I just keep playing. Sure enough, the next day I get a call from Carl at 6pm.

"Hello?"

"Hello, this is Carl from Comp-U-Tek. Is this Ray?"

"Yes."

"You made it back to Walmart?"

"Kinda."

"Kinda?"

"Well I tried carrying back most of the apples. 'Most' because I decided to keep 3 bags for the house. Anyway, as I was shuffling these apples back to Walmart, I kept getting stopped by people."

"What did they want?"

"Apples."

"Apples?"

"Apples."

"What did they want with the apples?"

"I don't know."

"I don't understand."

"People kept stopping me, wanting my apples."

"Really?"

"It was crazy. I just kept selling those apples like a street vendor. I made $247 before I got back to Walmart. Still managed to return 6 bags."

"That's incredible."

"I know, right?"

"So did you get the Apple cards?"

"Yes."

"Great!"

"And I put them in the slot in the computer, and it seems to be working much better."

"What do you mean?"

"I put the Apple cards in that slot in the front of the computer, then I opened up my game and finished it on the first try."

"What slot?"

"Come on, Carl. The one in the front. You should know what slot. You're the doctor."

"What?"

"I gave my computer the 2 Apples, and it cured the virus. I won my solitaire game, first try. That has never happened before. You're a genius."

"Have you been wasting my time?"

"No. Why would I waste your time allowing you to scam people out of real money for fake fixes?"

All I heard was a click. I shrugged. "Ok. Bye-bye."

Lower Interest Rates

I'm outside, on my break, walking around our building when my cell phone rings. I answer with, "Hello."

A man with a strong accent introduces himself as Mike and asks me if I would be interested in lowering my credit card debt.

"Sure," I say as I continue walking. I really could use someone to help keep the boredom of walking to a minimum.

Mike says, "What cards do you currently have? And do you know the interest rates?"

He thinks he's got me, but I've got him hooked, so I say, "Well, I have a couple of bank cards, a gas card, Walmart, Sears, Macy's, 7-11, two Circle K cards, Major Tom Auto works, Sacramento Zoo, Jiffy Lube, there are a few more. Oh, I also have Applebee's, Pizza Hut, Carl's Jr and Burger King. I don't have McDonalds because I like flame broiled burgers. Do you like flame broiled burgers?"

He just says, "I like hamburgers."

I reply, "Do you like flamed broiled or flat-top grilled?"

He says, "I like hamburgers in general," then tries to pull the conversation his way. "Do you know the interest rate you are paying for your cards?"

I pick a number, unreasonably big. "Most are like 30 to 35 percent."

"That is really high. We can help you get as low as 3.5% on all your cards."

I say, "That's incredible, sign me up," but then I hang up.

Still walking and smiling about the time I just wasted on Mike, my cell rings again, so I answer, "Hello?"

"Hi, this is Mike, and I think we got disconnected. Is this Ray?"

"Who is this?"

"It is Mike from Credit Connections. We were just talking about your credit cards."

I still have some time left on my break, so let's go with it. "I did not know you worked for Credit Connections. Do you know Carl?"

He answers, "No, I don't."

"How about Philip?"

"That name does not ring as bell."

"Martha?"

"No, sorry. About the credit cards…"

I continue pulling names <u>out of the air</u>. "Adam?"

"No, I don't know him either. We have about 200 people working here, and I am new."

"Well, if you run into any of them, tell them I said hello. Except Philip—he owes me $200 on a football bet and won't return my calls."

He tries to get control of the conversation. "Do you have the credit cards available?"

"I do. I need to go get them."

"I can wait."

I say, "Ok," as I finish my walk and head back inside to work. Mike is still patiently waiting for me.

He finally says, "How long will it take for you to get the cards?"

"I am getting them now."

Long pause.

"Do you have them?"

"Almost, I had to get my keys."

"Ok."

Long pause, and I'm now at my desk working…with him still on the line.

"Are we ready?"

"Not yet, there is a train."

"A train?"

"You have to wait. I can barely hear you." I wait about two minutes, then say, "Hello?"

"I thought you were going to get your cards."

"I am. I had to go get my keys."

"What did you need the keys for?"

"My car."

"Oh, the cards are in the car?"

"No, they are at home."

"Where are you now?"

"I'm almost home." Of course I'm really sitting at my desk, getting some work done, but I continue, "I had to wait for the train to pass. I'm so excited about lowering my interest rate on all my cards. You've really made my day."

"I am glad we can help you. This is what makes this job so enjoyable."

"Is Credit Connections hiring?"

"They are always hiring."

"Adam said he really liked working there."

"It is a great company."

"Crap," I say.

"What's wrong?"

"I left my house key on my desk at work. I can't get in the house. I am driving back to work now."

"Don't you have a hidden key?"

"Oh, I do have a hidden key. You are pretty smart. Turning around now. This is great."

"Glad I could help."

"Hmm, it's very quiet."

"What do you mean?"

"I have three dogs, and they usually start barking when I pull up."

"Is there a problem?"

"Hold on, let me get the key." I pause, then, "Huh? It's not here. I bet my niece came by and took the dogs to the park." I lean over and put a file in the cabinet...still working. I have to admit that I'm pretty good at multi-tasking.

"Does she have the key?"

"I assume she does."

"Is the park close?"

"I believe that it is open from 6 am to 10 pm, but I could be wrong. It might close at 11pm."

"No, is it close by?"

"Sorry, I thought you asked if it was closed."

"It's ok."

I wait.

He finally asks, "Is it close by?"

"Yes. I am walking over there now."

"How far away is it?"

"I would say less than two miles."

"Why don't you drive over?"

"Again another great idea. Let me walk back and get the car."

"Is this going to take much longer?"

"Not at all, just need to get the key from my niece."

"Sounds good."

I try a different tactic. "Are you married?"

"What?"

I ask again, "Are you married?"

"No. I have a girlfriend."

"How long have you been dating?"

"About 3 years."

"Cool. Ok, I see my niece, hold on." I pause for about two minutes, then continue, "Sorry that took so long. My dogs were so happy to see me. I just had to throw the ball for each of them a couple of times. Do you have any pets?"

"No, we can't have any animals in the apartment we live in."

"Did you have any pets growing up?"

"No, my mother did not like any animals."

"Wow, pets are so awesome. They teach responsibility to children. Do you have any children?"

"No, I do not have any children."

I keep up with the social questions. "How old are you?"

"I am 28."

"I'm 50."

He keeps trying to get back to the subject. "How are we doing on the credit cards?"

"I'm pulling up to the house now."

"Great."

"Ok, what do you need?"

"Let's start with the card that has the largest available credit."

"Ok, let me look. Hold on." I pause for about two more minutes.

"Ray?"

"Hold on, I am still looking up the info."

"What?"

"I am trying to log onto the accounts to see which card has the highest credit available."

"I can do that for you."

"How can you do that? You don't have the card numbers."

"You can give me the numbers, and I can see what the balances are and available credit."

"Why would I do that?"

"So I can lower your rates for you on all your cards."

"I not very comfortable giving you my card info over the phone."

"That's what we have been talking about the whole time. Lowering your interest rate."

I grin as I shake my head. "No, we talked about hamburgers, my friends that work there, pets, girlfriends, if you were married. We talked about more than just credit cards. I feel as though you weren't even listening to me. I am hurt. I thought you were a friend. Mike I'm sorry this relationship is just not going to work out."

I finally hang up the phone after 47 minutes had elapsed, a new personal record.

Magazines

I was eating lunch at my desk when my cell phone rang. I frowned as I picked it up. "Hello?"

"I know that you read magazines and do I have a spectacular deal for you."

"You do?" This guy called the wrong person. I don't read anything. Books, newspapers, magazines, directions to build something, recipes, I just don't read. I can. I just don't. It seems like a waste of time.

"My name is Eric and the company I work for, National Publications, has contracted with every magazine distributer to distribute their magazines at a drastically reduced rate."

"What rate?"

"Well, that depends on the magazine you choose and how long you want the subscription."

"Awesome."

"What is even better is that National Publications has allowed me to reduce it even further if you subscribe to more than one magazine."

"This just keeps getting better."

"Do you subscribe to many magazines?"

"I do. What kind of discount are we talking about?"

"Well, if you subscribe to 6 or more magazines, the discount could be as much as 90%."

"I'm interested, what now?" I say as I'm trying to figure out what magazine to ask him about.

"What magazines do you subscribe to currently?"

"I have quite a few magazines, and I just renewed some of them. What magazines do you have?"

"We have every magazine."

"Ok which ones?"

"Well, do you like sports?"

"I do. Which sports magazines do you have?"

"We carry every sports magazine."

"Like what?"

"Do you like Football?"

"No."

"Baseball?"

"No."

"Soccer, badminton, hockey, rugby?"

"No not really into those. What else?"

"Horse racing, auto racing, bicycle racing?"

"No, not really into racing…of any kind. Anything else?"

"Hiking, canoeing, swimming, skiing."

Ah. I know a little about skiing. I skied as a child, so I go with it. "Yes, I like skiing."

"We have Skiing, Down Hill Skiing, Snowboarding, Ski, Free Skier…"

"I already have all of those."

"Do you need to renew any of them?"

"No. Oh, wait. Do you have Bindings?"

"Bindings?"

"Yes Bindings. I have that one and it will expire next month. I really like that one."

"I don't see that one in our inventory. What is it about?"

"It talks about the manufacturing of bindings, the new technologies that are coming out, new material being used, and safety. You know, all the things a person would need to know about the manufacturing of bindings."

"I am afraid we don't carry that one. I am emailing my manager to contact them to become a distributer."

"Bummer. What else do you have?"

"Do you like fashion?"

"I do. What do you have?"

"We have every fashion magazine."

"Ok. Which ones?"

"Fashion World, Elle, Cosmo, In Style, Vogue, Allure…"

"I already have all of those."

"I see. Is there any that need the subscription renewed?"

Looking down at my dirty tennis shoes, I get an idea. "Not any of those. Do you have Shoes?"

"Shoes?"

"Yes, Shoes. That one will expire next month."

"Let me look. I don't see that one either."

"Oh."

"What is that magazine about?"

"It talks about the manufacturing of shoes, the new technologies that are coming out, new material being used, and safety. You know, all the things a person would need to know about the manufacturing of shoes and different footwear."

"Hmm. Let me email my manager again."

"What else do you have?"

"Do you have any hobbies?"

"I do. What hobby magazines do you have?"

"We have Railroad, Model Airplane, Crafting, Stamping, Coin Collecting, Dolls…"

I check my watch to see how long I've been on the phone—21 minutes, an idea… "Do you carry Watch?"

"Watch? "

"Yes, Watch."

"That one does not sound familiar. What is it about?"

"It talks about the manufacturing of watches, the new technologies that are coming out, new material being used, electronics, and, of course, safety. You know, all the things a person would need to know about the manufacturing of watches."

"I am going out on a limb here. I am willing to bet you are into manufacturing."

"I really like to see what is going on with the development of new technology."

"What do you do for a living may I ask?"

"I actually work as a janitor for one of the largest auto repair shops in our town. Our shop, Bill's Fast Auto Service, is number three in size. I tried to get a job at the number one and two shops, Auto Fix and We Care Auto, but they didn't need a janitor."

"Oh."

"Do you have Clubs Magazine? It is also going to expire next month."

"I don't see it."

"It talks about the manufacturing of golf clubs, the new technologies that are coming out, new material being used, and safety. You know, all the things a person would need to know about the manufacturing of golf clubs."

"Where did you find all the manufacturing magazines?"

"On line. I searched for things that were interesting to me."

"Wow."

"What other magazines do you have?" I keep him going.

"We have Automobile magazines. "

"Like what?"

"Car and Driver, Auto Week, Motor Trend, Popular Mechanics, Road and Track, Muscle Machines…"

"I have all of those. Just renewed them, too. Do you have Nuts and Bolts?"

"Nut and Bolts, Let me look. I don't see that one."

"Darn. The subscription is about to expire."

"Let me guess it's about—"

"The manufacturing of nuts and bolts, the new technologies that are coming out, new material being used, and safety. You know, all the things a person would need to know about the manufacturing of nuts and bolts."

"I can see where this is going."

"Where is this going?"

"You want manufacturing magazines."

"I do."

"I am looking right now at our entire collection of magazines. I know we have to have some."

"Can you sort by type of magazine?"

"I can, but Manufacturing is not one of the choices. This is so frustrating."

"I bet. You haven't be able to find any of the magazines I need."

"I am emailing my manager right now."

I finish eating my lunch and another magazine popped into my head. "Eric, do you have any cooking magazines?"

"We do. There are a ton of those."

"What ones do you carry?"

"Well, we have Living, Taste of Home, Bon Appetite, Food & Wine, Fine Cooking…"

"Do you have Pots and Pans?"

"Pots and Pans?"

"Yes, it talks about the manufacturing of Pots and Pans, the new technologies that are coming out, new material being used, and safety. You know, all the things a person would need to know about the manufacturing of Pots and Pans."

"I'm sure it does. Is your subscription about to expire?"

"Holy cow, it is. Did you find that one?"

"No."

I sigh…loudly. "I have given you *six* magazines that are about to expire, and you haven't been able to do a thing for me."

"I'm starting to believe that these magazines don't really exist."

"That is not true. They do exist. They are real. Um, Eric, can you hold on a moment? I need to refill my coffee, and Santa just showed up with a fresh brew."

"Santa? This is crap you have wasted my time."

"It's not my fault. The Easter Bunny and Tooth Fairy have had a gun to my head. They made do it."

All I heard was a click.

EarthLink

I was watching TV and my home phone rang. I reached over and answered. "Hello?"

"Hello, this is Kelly from EarthLink and have we got a deal for you."

"Who is this?"

"This is Kelly from EarthLink and have we got a deal for you."

"Tell me more."

"What is your name?"

"My name is Ray, What is your name?"

"My name is Kelly from EarthLink."

"Oh yea that right you told me that before."

"Have you heard of EarthLink?"

"No, I haven't."

"Well we have an amazing deal for you."

"Please tell me more about it."

"Right now we are offering EarthLink at an amazing price."

I grin. "Say it isn't so."

"Ray, we are offering EarthLink for half off the regular price of $19.99. You can get EarthLink for 1 year at the incredibly low price of only $9.99 a month."

"I love it. Sign me up."

"Great. Let me get some information from you."

"Ok."

"First, let me get your name."

"It's Ray."

"Thank you, Ray. Can I get your last name?"

"Sure it's S…wait, what do I do with EarthLink?"

"You connect to the internet."

"Great I like that."

"Ok, your last name?"

"It's S…wait, I don't have a computer."

"You don't have a computer?"

"No, sorry."

"Are you going to get a computer?"

"I am now. I am going to have EarthLink. I can't pass up this deal. What was it again?"

"It was half off the regular price of $19.99. You can get EarthLink for 1 year at the incredibly low price of only $9.99 a month."

"That's right. So I need to go buy a computer."

"Great. So your last name is?"

"Yes. It's Sh…wait, I'm having a problem with this."

"What is the problem?"

"Well…When will this EarthLink be available?"

"As so as we get all your information entered into the system."

"Great."

"So, Ray, your last name is?"

"It's Sh…Kelly?"

"Yes, Ray."

"Why would I get EarthLink before I get the computer?"

"That is a great question, Ray. You know, we can hold off on billing you for EarthLink for thirty days."

"That is great Sign me up."

"So your last name is…"

"It's Sh…You know, Kelly, I'm still a little confused."

"Yes, Ray. What can I do to help with the confusion?"

"If I were to buy EarthLink now, it would be like buying tires for a car that I don't own yet. Does that make sense?"

"Yes completely."

"I mean the size wheel, the size tire, the type of tread. It might be a car or truck. It's just crazy to buy tires for a vehicle that you don't own yet. Right?"

"I understand. You *would* be crazy to buy tires like that. However, EarthLink works on all computers. There will not be any doubt that it won't work."

"This sounds too good to be true."

"No, Ray. This is a real deal. A great deal. And you are one of the lucky ones to get this offer."

"Today has be a great day. I found a four leaf clover in the front yard, and as I was walking out the street to get the mail, my neighbor Ted's black cat was walking and was going to cross my path, but stopped, and he saw me and turned around and walked the other direction. And then I get a call form you offering me EarthLink for... What was the deal again?"

"It is half off the regular price of $19.99. You can get EarthLink for 1 year at the incredibly low price of only $9.99 a month."

"That's right. Can you believe that? How can someone get so lucky?"

"You are extremely lucky. So your last name is?"

"It's Sh...You know, Kelly, I'm not even sure what I would do with EarthLink."

"What do you mean?"

"What do I do with EarthLink?"

"You can surf the web."

"I don't swim."

"No surfing the web is looking up information about different things on the web."

"Like what?"

"Anything."

"Give me an example."

"You could find out how to make Baked Alaska."

"What is that? "

"It is an ice cream dessert that gets baked."

"That sounds yummy. What else?"

"You could look up vacation destinations."

"Like where?"

"Pick a spot."

"Trona."

"Trona?"

"Yes, Trona."

"Where is that?"

"It is a little town in California that has a chemical plant."

"Yes you could find information about Trona on the web."

"Great."

"So, Ray, your last name is S...?"

"Yes. Its Sh... What else can I do?"

"Besides surfing the web?"

"Yes"

"Well you can send email."

"I've heard of that."

"Good, it is amazing."

"How does it work?"

"Well you send a letter to someone electronically."

"That sounds good, but how do you do that?"

"Well first you type a letter—"

"Wait, you what?"

"You type a—"

"I can't do that."

"Can't do what?"

"I can't type a letter."

"Why can't you type a letter?"

"I don't have any hands."

"You don't have any hands?"

"No. I lost them."

"I'm so sorry."

"Well actually not only are my hands gone, but from the elbow down. So I don't have any wrists or forearms either."

"That is terrible."

"Tell me about it. Have you ever tried to wipe your butt with your elbow? I would venture to say that you haven't. It's really difficult to do."

"I bet. I'm so sorry."

"So, Kelly, as you can imagine, a computer hasn't been a high priority for me."

"I understand."

"The deal with EarthLink. What was it again?"

"It is half off the regular price of $19.99. You can get EarthLink for 1 year at the incredibly low price of only $9.99 a month."

"That's right. It sounds too good to pass up. I'm always looking for a good deal, but a computer…it has me a little confused on how it would work for me."

"Ray, I understand completely. Did you know that there are programs out there that will do voice to text for you?"

"Get out. Seriously"

"I'm not kidding."

"That would be great. Then EarthLink would make sense."

"Ok then. Your last name is?"

"It's Sh…oh, wait, Kelly, I need to go poop. I'm going to need to do this at another time," I said as I hung up the phone.

Dell

My wife called me and said that she just ordered a new Dell Computer. That bothers me as I have been out of work for almost a year, and there's not much I can do from here. I'm 4 hours away and just interviewed for a job with the State of California, so I'm not even certain that I am going to have any work yet, and she spends $2500 on a new Dell Computer. When I complain, she tells me that it is ok. She charged it to her Aunt's card, so won't hit our credit.

"We still have to pay her each month," I said. "We can't afford that. I'm going to call and cancel the order."

With some reluctance she agreed that that would be the best thing to do, so I make the call to Dell.

"Dell customer service, this is Dena. How may I help you?"

"Hi, Dena."

"May I have your name and account number?"

"I don't know what it is."

"You don't know your name?"

"Sorry. Ray."

"Thank you, Ray. I can look it up by your phone number."

"Ok."

"What is the phone number associated with this account?"

"I'm not sure. My wife just placed an order for a computer. Maybe 20 minutes ago."

"Let's look under her phone number."

"Ok. It's 760-555-1212."

"I believe I have it here in front of me. What is her name?"

"Mary."

"And her date of birth?"

"Its 4/11/69."

"Ok, what can I do for you?"

"I want to cancel the order."

"I sorry. Once the order has been put into production, it cannot be cancelled."

"It just was placed 20 minutes ago. How can it be in production already?"

"This is Dell. We have state of the art equipment. Orders are handled with top priority. Our customers are important to us. We here at Dell strive to make you happy."

"Do you know what would make me happy, Dena?"

"What is that, Ray?"

"Cancel my order."

"Again, I'm sorry, but once an order has been placed it cannot be canceled."

"That doesn't make any sense." I shake my head and continue. "So, what did she order?"

"Mary ordered a Pentium 625XPS with 500GB Hard Drive, 8MB RAM Memory, 26" Photo-Chromatic Monitor, Wireless mouse and keyboard, LaserJet XPS Pro Printer, and Windows with Microsoft Office Pro. The total is $2478.35."

"The total is $2500! Are you kidding me?"

"No it is only $2478.35. And that includes delivery."

"I don't want it."

"May I ask why?"

"My wife did not consult me about the computer. I wouldn't have chosen that model."

"What would you have chosen?"

"I wanted the Dell 895XPS with the 1TB Hard Drive and 32GB RAM."

"We can make that change for you."

"Wait. You can make a change on an order that has already sent through your state of the art computer system."

"Yes we can. Like I said, it is state of the art. Best in the country."

"So you can change an order that is in production to something else, but cannot cancel an order."

"That is correct."

"Strange. For being so state of the art, it seems like you would have that ability."

"Nope, we don't."

"Dena, is there any way that I can speak to a supervisor?"

"Certainly, let see if one is available. Can you hold for me please?"

"I sure can." I am a little upset, but not all is lost. I am pretty good at talking to people, so I'm betting I can get it taken care of. While I wait, I sit on the couch and watch the Price is Right.

"Ray?"

"Yes."

"I'm sorry. A manager is not available at this time."

"Why?"

"There is not one available."

"There is not *one* manager available."

"Again, I am sorry. They are in a meeting."

"Ok, I'll wait."

"What?"

"I'll wait."

"It may be a while. We can call you back."

"No. I'll wait." I hum as I watch TV for a minute or so... "Is one available now?" I said to Dena.

"No. Like I said earlier, they are in a meeting."

"Ok, I'll wait." I sat up and yelled at the TV, "No, pick the tooth paste. How stupid." Turning back to the phone, I said, "This woman thought that a can of Campbell's Chicken Noodle Soup was more expensive than a tube of Crest Toothpaste." I pause. "Is a manager available, now?"

"No. I have work to do. Can we disconnect this call?"

"No. I am still waiting to speak to a manager." I continued humming and commenting on the show. "This woman has to putt from 8 feet. There is no way she is going to make it. Oh, oh, oh…nope she missed. Wait. No way. This game isn't Hole in One—It is Hole in One or Two. She gets another try. Come on, you got this." I turn back to the phone. "Is there a manager available yet?"

"Not yet."

"Go, go, go, go, go! Ah, she missed again. This is one of my favorite shows. Do you like The Price is Right?"

"It's ok"

"I love it. If I were on the show, I'd win all the games. I'm really good at guessing the price of different items. I'll bet that I could get the price right every time. Oh, now I get it…It's The Price is Right. Too cool. Is a manager available yet?"

"I am sorry. There is not a manager available yet."

"Ok, I'll wait." I comment more. "The contestants are getting ready to spin the big wheel. If I were to spin the wheel, Dena, I would jump up and pull it as hard as I could. Make it go around as many times as possible. The three that are spinning right now look pretty wimpy. Sara is spinning first. It barely made it around one time. She landed on 35 cents. Sara is spinning again. Is the manager available?"

"No, Not yet."

"Ok, I'll wait. Sara landed on 45 cents this time. She has 80 cents total. Dena, did you know that contestant that is closest to one dollar without going over will go to the showcase showdown?"

"I knew that."

"Isn't that awesome. David is spinning now. Too cool, he jumped up and tried to spin the wheel really hard. Look at it go. Oh, yea, you can't see it. Believe me when I say it's spinning. Wow. Go, go, go, go. It stopped on 85 cents. He's stopping, not going to spin again, and now he's the leader. Speaking of leaders, is there a manager available?"

"No, not yet. Is there any way we can call you back?"

"No thanks, I'll wait. Now its golf girl spinning. I missed her name. Going, going, going. 20 cents. Alice is her name. Alice is going to spin again. Here she goes. Spinning and, and, and, and, and the wheel stopped on 40 cents. David is the winner and heading to the showcase showdown. I hope he wins. My brother's best friend growing up was named David. Wouldn't that be great if he won?"

"Ray, my manager has just come in. I will be transferring you to her. Her name is Brenda."

"Thank you, Dena. It has been a pleasure talking with you."

"Thank you, Ray. Here is Brenda."

The voice on the other end changes, so I know it's not just Dena trying to get rid of me. "Hello is this Ray?"

"Yes it is. Who is this?"

"My name is Brenda and I am the Sales manager."

"Are you a decision making manager?"

"Yes. How can I help you?"

"Well, are you able to see our account?"

"Yes, I can see that you ordered a Pentium 625XPS with 500GB Hard Drive, 8MB RAM Memory, 26" Photo-Chromatic Monitor, Wireless mouse and keyboard, LaserJet XPS Pro Printer, and software Windows with Microsoft Office Pro. The total is $2478.35."

"Yes, my wife ordered that. We don't need it. I would like to cancel the order."

"Not a problem. Hold on one moment while I enter the cancelation codes."

"Thank you, Brenda."

"Ok, all done. Ray, when you are looking for a new computer please consider us. Remember that we are Dell. We have state of the art equipment. Orders are handled with top priority. Our customers are important to us. We here at Dell strive to make you happy. We are here for you."

"Thanks, Brenda."

All she heard was a click.

Sorry you died...again

My cellphone rings. "This is Ray."
"May I speak to Annie?"
"Who is this?"
"This is Carol. Is Annie available?"
"Carol who?"
"Carol Whitmore."
"This is Ray."
"May I speak to Annie?"
"What is this regarding?"
"This is a personal matter. I need to speak to her directly. Is she available?"
"She is not available. We have been happily married for three years; however, she has mentioned that she might be interested in experimenting with ano—"
"No, I'm sorry. It is not that kind of call."
"Sure it is. You asked if my happily married wife was available. I responded she is not, but might be interested. Do you have a picture you could send us and what ideas you have?"
"I am calling from Wells Fargo."
"North Dakota?"
"What?"
"Wells Fargo, North Dakota?"
"No, Wells Fargo the bank."
"Oh, and what do you need?"
"Is Annie available?"
"There you go again. Do you have any pictures you can send us?"
"That is not what this call is about."
"What is it about?"
"I need to talk to Annie."
"I see. If you think that the two of you are going to do something without me, I can tell you it's not going to happen. She

is happily married, and though we have talked about experimenting, I was always involved."

"Ray, I am not interested in your wife like that."

"Why not? She is beautiful, funny, a joy to be around, super fun in the sack."

"I need to talk to Annie."

"Why?"

"Like I said it is a personal matter."

"Are you having an affair with my wife?"

"No, I am not having an affair with your wife."

"Why not?"

"That is not what the call is about."

"You said that it is a personal call."

"It is."

"How long have you been seeing my wife?"

"I am not seeing your wife."

"Stop. Ok, we were having troubles. I knew she needed a friend, I just never thought that she would do this without me. I am so hurt."

"Nothing happened between your wife and I."

"I don't believe you. You call here and ask to have a personal conversation with her. You won't tell me the details. You are having an affair with her."

"I am not having an affair with your wife."

"Stop lying."

"There has been a complete misunderstanding."

"You can't fix this. I am done." I hang up, click. Then call my ex-wife and let her know that Wells Fargo called again. I told her the conversation I just had, so if she ever talks to Carol, she can continue the conversation.

The next day my cellphone rings again. "This is Ray."

"Is Annie there?"

"Who is this?"

"This is Adam. I am calling from Wells Fargo. Is Annie there?"

I start to cry and weep on the phone.

"Is there a problem?"

Still weeping, I say that she just passed away from a golf accident.

"What happened?"

I remembered a story I'd heard so adapted it for this situation. "Well we were playing golf at Stone Ridge (weep, weep), and I sliced a shot into the woods."

"Sliced?"

"That's when you hit the ball and it goes to the right really bad."

"I see."

"Anyway, I found my ball, and I was close to the green, but a barn was between my ball and the green. (weep, weep) I could try to hit the ball over the barn, but that was really risky."

"I don't understand."

"Please, let me finish."

"I'm sorry, go ahead."

"My wife suggested that we open the barn doors and I shoot right through. (weep, weep)"

"Sounds good."

"It was a great idea. I used my 3 iron to punch through the barn, but the ball hit the door jam. It came straight back and hit my wife in the temple. (weep weep)"

"Oh my. That is awful."

"It is. I ended up getting a 9 on that hole."

"What about your wife?"

"She's dead." Click.

I called my ex-wife to let her know that Wells Fargo had called and that she had died. She thanked me for the info.

The next day my cellphone rings again. "This is Ray."

"Is Annie there?"

"Who is this?"

"This is Annie. Is Annie there?"

"You are on the phone."

"No I need to speak to Annie."
"Can you hear me?"
"Yes I can."
"Ok, go ahead with your questions."
"What?"
"Annie is listening."
"I need to speak to her."
"Is your name Annie?"
"Yes it is."
"Go ahead."
"Go ahead and what?"
"Speak."
"Is Annie on the phone?"
"Yes."
"May I speak to her?"
"You are speaking to her. She is always here."
"May I talk to her?"
"You can. I talk to her all the time."
"I need Annie on the phone."
"You want me to put some of her on the phone?"
"What?"
"All I have are ashes."
"What?"
"She died."
"I am so sorry."
"Thanks." Click

I called my ex-wife to let her know that Wells Fargo had called and that she had died…again.

The Loan

My cellphone rings. It looks like the call is coming in from Texas. I answer, "Hello this is Ray."

"Hello, this is Johnathan. I am calling from Credit Services. Is this Ray?"

"Yes it is."

"I wanted to let you know that we have an incredible offer available for you."

"Ok, what is it?"

"We have loans available at very low interest rates…between 2 and 4%."

"That's incredible."

"Would you be interested in a loan?"

"I would."

"Great, how much are you looking for?"

"How about $500,000?"

"How much?"

"$500,000."

"We can do that."

"Great." I hang up. I get a call a few minutes later (from Texas again). "Hello?"

"Hello. It's Johnathan. I believe that we were just disconnected."

"No, I hung up."

"I thought you wanted the loan."

"I do." I hang up. Again my phone rings. "Hello?"

"Hello, this is Johnathan. We keep getting disconnected. I need to get some information from you before we can process the loan."

"Well, I'm 6'3", about 250 pounds, my hair used to be blonde but now it's gone. Ha, ha. I just rhymed. Anyway, people say I am witty and very fast with comments and come backs."

"No I need personal information."

"Ok, well I have two brothers and a sister. I have been married four times. I have 2 children, 3 dogs, and 2 cats."

"Not that kind of personal information."

"Oh, sorry. I sucked my thumb until I was 13. I lost my virginity when I was sixteen—"

"No, I need personal *financial* information."

"Oh, what do you need?"

"Well first we need your full name."

"What would the payments be on $500,000?"

"I first need to enter the information into the computer to see what the payments would be."

"But if I can't afford the payment, you might be wasting my time."

"I can't tell you what the payments would be until the computer gives it to me."

"Give me a rough guess."

"Let me see…about how much money do you make each month?"

"It varies."

"What do you mean it varies?"

"It depends on how many days I work each month. I can sometimes collect between $250 and $400 a day."

"How many days do you work?"

"Some weeks I work every day. Most weeks I collect maybe 3 or 4 days."

"So that works out to about $7000 a month."

"That seems close, but I'm not sure. So the payments would be…?"

"I am still not sure. I need to enter more information."

"Just a guess?"

"I don't know."

"Something I can tell my wife."

"I don't know, maybe somewhere between $2000 and $2400 a month."

"Great I can do that." I hang up. Again my phone rings moments later. I don't answer it. Two days later I receive a call from Wisconsin. "Hello, this is Ray."

"Hello, this is Johnathan. I am calling from Credit Services. Do you remember me?"

"I do. Where are you located?"

"Our company is located in Texas."

"Why does it show that you are calling from Wisconsin?"

"I don't know."

"Ok." I am going to string this guy on for as long as I can.

"We were talking about the $500,000 loan."

"Yes, I am so excited about the loan. I told my wife, and she can't believe it."

"That is wonderful."

"Thanks." I hang up, but, as expected, my phone rings. I don't answer it. A day later, I receive a call from Texas. "Hello, this is Ray."

"Hello, this is Johnathan. I am calling from Credit Services. Do you remember me?"

"I do."

"Good. We were talking about your $500,000 loan."

"Yes. This is wonderful. We have started looking for a new house to buy."

"Very nice."

"Nothing like this ever happens to me. We finally get to move into a new home."

"I am excited for you also. I promise that you and your wife will be really happy with this loan."

"Thanks." I hang up. Again my phone rings. "Hello, this is Ray."

"Hello, this is Johnathan. I believe that we were disconnected."

"No, I hung up. I thought we were done."

"No, I need to get some information from you."

"Ok."

"Do you have an email address?"

"I don't."

"Does your wife have an email address?"

"I believe she does. Let me check." I hang up. My phone rings. A call from Texas. I don't answer it. A day later Wisconsin calls me. "Hello, this is Ray."

"Hello, this is Johnathan."

"Hello."

"Did you find out about your wife's email address?"

"She can't find it."

"What do you mean she can't find it?"

"She says she put it in the glove compartment, but now it's gone. She even accused me of taking it. I asked her what in the world I was going to do with her address. She is still mad at me."

"Is there anybody else who might have an email address you can use?"

"I believe my brother has one. Actually I am pretty sure he has one, and he might let me use it. Let me call him." I hang up. Three days later Wisconsin calls. "Hello, this is Ray."

"Hello, this is Johnathan."

"Hello."

"Were you able to get a hold of your brother?"

"No, he is on vacation."

"Well we could mail the application to you. This will take a bit longer."

"That would be fine. I believe we have found the perfect house to buy."

"We are on our way to that new home for you and your wife, Ray."

"We still can't believe it. To actually cook a meal in our kitchen. Shower in an actual shower, not a gas station bathroom sink. This is truly amazing."

"Where do I send the application to?"

"We are currently staying at the Chevron on the corner of 16th and Douglas."

"What? Do you own a home now?"

"No. We are buying one right now."

"How are you doing that?"

"With the loan from you."

"We haven't given you a loan yet."

"You haven't? Why not?"

"You have to be approved. We need some documents from you in order to process the application."

"What documents do you need?"

"We need a copy of your driver's license, a copy of a utility bill, and we need to verify your income."

"Ok, I can do that."

"What do you do for a living, Ray?"

"As I said before, I am a collector."

"What do you collect?"

"Cans."

"Cans?"

"Yes, cans."

"What kind of cans?"

"Aluminum cans. I collect them almost every day."

"You collect aluminum cans for a living?"

"Yeah, and I'm really good at it. Probably the best in our community. I have all the hot spots. I know the collection times so I can get there before the sanitation department. Some of the local bars also collect for me."

"I am sorry, Ray, but I believe that this is not going to work out."

"You said that you were going to give me a loan. I told my wife, the kids, the dogs, and the cats that we were moving into a new home. Now you're telling me that you're not going to give me the loan?"

"We cannot approve you for any loan with this information."

"That is bull. We've already found the perfect home to buy. It is a single-wide, fixer-upper trailer right next to the highway. It has a swing set in the back yard already and a stock pile of pallets that I can burn for heat in the winter."

"What, what are you talking about?"

"How on earth can you promise a person something like that, build up their hopes and dreams, and then shatter them at the last minute? I bet you look for children with ice cream cones just so you can knock them out of their hands. You probably drive with your blinker on, too. You're the kind of person that puts tape on the feet of cats." I laugh. "That *is* kinda funny, though." I turn serious. "Johnathan you are not a very nice man." I hang up. I have yet to get another call from Texas or Wisconsin or Johnathan.

This telephone call actually lasted just over six weeks. I went through three different people at that company—all with the same name: Johnathan. Apparently, they thought I couldn't tell that they were different people. I even created a fake email address to send a fake hand written receipt from a fake recycling center for 164 pounds of aluminum cans to verify my income. Almost seven weeks. A new personal best.

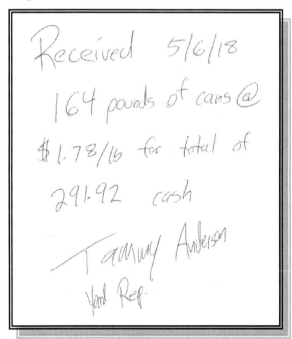

Health Insurance

I was sitting on the couch at my girlfriend's house when her cellphone rang. She looked at it and said, "It's a telemarketer. I hate these calls."

"Let me have the phone," I said. In a high girlish voice I answered, "Hello?"

"Hello, this is Megan, and I am calling from United Health Care."

In the girlish voice, I talk to Megan. "Hello."

"We are offering to residents of California the opportunity to acquire a low cost health insurance."

"That sounds great."

"Wonderful, if you would like, I can give you a quote about how affordable our insurance can be for you."

Still in my girlish voice I say, "That sounds really good. What about my children. Can they be on the plan too?"

"Of course, this plan offers something for everyone."

"I like it already."

"Good, let's get started."

"Ok."

"What is your name?"

"Jessica Matters."

"Got it."

"How about your date of birth?"

"04/11/75."

"You are an Aries, so am I," she said.

"Wow."

"How would you consider your health to be right now?"

"Well, I am alive, does that count?"

"Yes, that happens to be a prerequisite. Do you have any aliments?"

"What do you mean?"

"Are you sick?"

"I am."

"What seems to be the problem?"

"Well, it makes me sick that I can't get my children to do their homework. They think that I am going to do it for them every day. I can't. Some of the problems are just too difficult."

"No, I am wondering if you are feeling medically sick."

"Oh, I recently went to the doctor because I hurt all over. Every time I touched my ear it hurt. When I touched my left wrist it hurt. My right side, both knees, even my left big toe hurt when I touched it."

"Oh, my."

Still in my girlish voice, I continue, "My front teeth, my belly button, it really hurt to comb my hair. It even hurt to open my purse. I hurt all over."

"What did the doctor determine was wrong?"

"Well after some extensive research and testing, he figured out that the pointer finger on my right hand was broken."

"At least they found the problem."

"Now I have a splint on my right finger, and I don't hurt all over anymore." *Are you kidding me*, I'm thinking. *This lady is really desperate for a sale.*

"So otherwise do you feel that you are in pretty good health?"

"I do, except for the fungus."

"What fungus?"

"There is a fungus that is growing in the backyard, and I believe that it might be making us sick."

"Why would the fungus be making you sick?"

"It's growing all over the place."

"What kind of fungus is it?"

"Some kind of mushroom. I heard that they might be poisonous."

"Are you eating them?"

"No."

"They can't harm you if you are not eating them."

"What about the pores?"

"The pores?"

"Yes the pores from the mushrooms."

"Spores."

"What?"

"Mushrooms have spores."

"What are spores? These mushrooms pour out seeds that are poisonous."

"No mushrooms have 'spores.' "

"Are they poisonous?"

"They could be, but I doubt it. Just don't eat them."

"Can they be airborne?"

"Really, the mushrooms are not a problem." She sighs. "Let me ask you some more questions."

I start to deepen my voice. "Not a problem. Go ahead."

"Do you or any of your family have any history of mental illness?"

"I have an uncle that we all believe is crazy. Is that what you mean?"

"Why do you think he is crazy?"

"He likes to skydive, bungie jump, cliff dive, hang glide. He even has pet rattlesnakes. He's crazy."

"Has he been diagnosed as mentally incompetent?"

"I don't think so."

"We will assume that the answer to that question is 'no'."

"Ok."

"Any heart disease that you know of?"

"My heart was broken about 3 years ago when my ex-husband decided that he wanted to be married to his job more than his family. My heart hasn't completely healed."

"That is not heart disease. We will put down 'no' for that question also."

"What about cigarettes?"

My voice continued getting deeper. "Which brand?"

"Which brand?"

"Which brand do you want to know about?"

"I don't need to know about brands. Do you smoke?"

"I do."

"How long have you been smoking?"

I let my voice get even deeper. "I started when I was 13, maybe October that year. That's 88, so 98, 2008, 9, 10, 11, 12, 13, 14. Almost 26 years. 26 in October. Its July now. So roughly 25 years 9 months."

"Your voice is changing." She finally noticed.

"That happens when I talk for long periods of time. The doctor said it was some sort of proactive emphysema. It attacks the vocal cords."

"I have not heard of that. "

"Yes, it really made it difficult when I was in the choir at church."

"Why is that?"

"Normally I would sing with the sopranos, but if we had a concert we were doing," my voice got deeper, "I would move down as the concert went on."

"That is different."

"Yep. I had to learn many parts. I had solos as a soprano, alto, tenor, baritone, and even as a bass. All in the same concert."

"I don't know what to say."

"My vocal range starts out high and over time gets deeper," my voice got even deeper, "and deeper."

"Unfortunately, this insurance is not available to you if you have ever been a smoker."

"Is there any way we can put down 'no' for this question also?"

"I don't think so."

"Why not? We did for those other questions. My crazy uncle, my broken heart. How about you say that I only smoke when I'm on fire?"

"We can't do that."

"Yes, you can."

"No I can't."

"Come on. What if I quit next month?"
"No."
"Next week?"
"No."
"Tomorrow?"
"I can't do it, Jessica."
"How about just one more cigarette? I'll quit right after that."
"No."
"Ok, I don't smoke anymore. I just quit."
"That's not going to work."
"Come on, Megan, work with me here. I just quit smoking, and you can't offer me anything?"
"You are not eligible for this insurance. I'm sorry."
"Do you have any other insurance?"
"No, I work for United Health Care."
"Homeowner's?"
"No."
"Auto?"
"No. I need to go."
"Renters?"
"Sorry."
"Pet?"
"Have a great day."
"Travel?" All I heard was a click.

The IRS

My cell phone rang and I answered it. "Hello, this is Ray" but it was only a recording: "This is the IRS, and we have discovered that you are seriously delinquent in your back taxes. An internal audit has determined that you owe us money. If you do not want the cops to come by your home in the next 24hrs to arrest you, you must call (202) 389-9820." By the way this is the real phone number they called me from.

Not wanting the "cops" to come by my home in the next 24hs, I decided I had better give them a call.

I dial and hear the phone ringing. "IRS Collection Department, this is Mr. Stevens. Is this Ray?"

"Yes it is. How did you know that?"

"We have your phone number."

"How did you get my number? I haven't given it to you yet."

"Our computer system recognized you when you called in."

"It did?"

"Yes."

"What am I wearing?"

"I'm sorry?"

"What am I wearing? If the system can recognize me, what am I wearing?"

"It's not like that. The system recognizes your phone number."

"I see."

"How can I help you?"

"Well I received a call that said the cops were going to come by and arrest me in the next 24hrs."

"Yes that is true, but because you called, we will be able to stop the cops from coming out to your home."

"That's good. I don't want the cops coming over here. I have too many guns, pit bulls, and fighting chickens, and I have a chop shop in my garage. If they showed up I'd go to jail, and I don't want that. I bet you can understand that."

"I do. That would be terrible. Let's get this IRS problem behind us."

"Sounds good to me. What do you need from me?"

"Well we show that you owe $300 dollars on—"

"Just $300? Oh, no problem. What do I do?"

"Well, the $300 is just the collection fees."

"Oh, so what do I owe you?"

"It shows that you owe $1300 for the—"

"Just $1300? That plus the $300, so $1600. No problem. Can I use my debit card?"

"Well, Ray, the $1300 is for one quarter. The total for the year would be $5200 plus the $300."

"Ok $5500, that's easy. What do I need to do?"

"Ray, I am glad that you are so willing to get this issue cleared up."

"I feel a lot better now. I thought it might be more money than that."

"Well, I see that there are a few other charges here."

"What? Ohhhh, shoot. Give it to me."

"I'm sorry, Ray, its $17,500."

"That's all? I thought it was more than that."

"Ray, that would clear just one of the accounts."

"How many are there?"

"Let me look. Can I place you on a brief hold?"

"Please, I want to get this taken care of."

"No problem. Hold on."

I'd bet that this guy is doing backflips about his luck in finding such a sucker. I'm smiling just wondering how high I can get this to go.

"Ray?"

"Yes, I am still here."

"Good, I did a search on all your accounts. It is still searching, but I believe that we have all of them here now. There are three more totaling $68,950, so the total with collections is $91,950."

"No problem. I made that last weekend with the chicken fights. What do I need to do?"

"We need to get this paid."

"Can you take a credit card, wire transfer, debit card? I just want this taken care of. Possibly today. I don't need the cops over here tonight. We have a really big dog fight. Lots of cash here. Can I give you guys cash?"

"We cannot take cash, but you can pay through Western Union."

"Perfect, I have one of those nearby."

"Great."

"So do I just send it to the IRS?"

"No, that won't work."

"Ok, what do I do?"

"Well, we are the collection department for the IRS."

"I see."

"And all money is sent here to be put into your correct account."

"Perfect."

"The best way to do it would be to send it to me, so I can apply it to the correct accounts. There are five accounts, and we know how much needs to go into each account."

"Ok, what do I do?"

"Western Union is the best bet. There are fees with them, but we will absorb that since you are paying today. We will subtract the amount in fees paid from the total."

"How do you do that?"

"Do you have the cash available right now?"

"I do."

"Perfect. Take the $91,950 to Western Union and send the maximum amount they allow you to send. They have a limit of how much can be sent, so you'll have to send multiple partial payments to make the total. Send the transactions to me, Irving Stevens @ Irving Ryan Stevens Collections."

"Why am I sending it to Irving Ryan Stevens Collections?"

"I am IRS Collections."

"Oh that makes perfect sense."

"There are so many people that owe the IRS money that they have hired independent companies to collect the additional charges that are owed the IRS. We then apply the charges to the correct accounts."

"How do you get paid?"

"I work for the IRS. I get paid for the work I do. I am an hourly employee."

"That must suck. All that money coming in, and you don't get any of it."

"It does. Sometimes I wish that I could keep it, but that would be wrong."

"I bet."

"It really makes me happy that I stop cops from coming to people's homes to arrest them."

"Thanks for looking out for the welfare of people. So what do I do again?"

"Take the cash to Western Union and send the maximum to me, Irving Stevens @ Irving Ryan Stevens Collections."

"Ok, then what?"

"They will charge you a fee."

"I thought you said I don't have to pay any fees."

"You don't. Pay the fee, and send the maximum amount again."

"What?"

"You may need to send a few transactions. That's ok. We will absorb all the fees. Just keep sending the maximum. When you get to the end, send what is left over. Do not bring more than what is owed. That way you only pay $91,950."

"Oh, so the last payment will have all the fees reduced off of what I am paying?"

"Yes, now you have it."

"That will be easy."

"So, Ray, be careful when you are heading over to Western Union. You don't want to get ripped off. Also be careful about talking to strangers. They might try to scam you."

"How would they do that?"

"They might try to sell you something, or just steal your money. You want to make sure you get this paid, so the cops don't come by in the next 24 hrs."

"I will, I will. The dog fight is a big money maker, and I don't want to jeopardize my chop shop either."

"Good."

"I am on my way right now. Thanks, Irving."

"No problem, Ray. And thank *you*." I could almost hear his grin as he rubbed his hands together in anticipation.

A New Credit Card

My cell phone rings, and I answer it. "Hello, this is Ray."

"Hi, this is Lisa, and I am calling from Aztec Credit Cards. Would you be interested in opening an account with Aztec?"

"I may. What can you offer me?"

"Well, Ray, we are offering home owners a credit card that can be attached to the equity of your home. That way you don't feel the pinch of credit crunch."

"Credit crunch?"

"Yes, credit crunch. It is an industry term that refers to all the payments that a person has to make each month. When you bite down on an apple, you hear a crunch right?"

"Yes."

"That is the same thing."

"Oh, so we are going to take a bite out of the payments."

"You could say that."

"That is what I just said, but ok…" I inhale, "We are going to take a bite out of the payments."

"Yes kinda. By attaching this card to the equity in your home, you can choose not to make payments if you wish."

"Are you kidding me? That's awesome. Sometimes I don't have the money to make all the payments. That would help me out a bunch."

"Ray, we can combine all of your cards to this card and really save you some money."

"I love it."

"Shall we get started?"

"Sure, but first I was wondering if you knew what the interest rate on the card would be."

"Currently we are at 31%."

"31% are you kidding me? That's is incredible. My other cards are like 39 to 46%. 31% is outstanding."

"31% is an amazing rate. I am glad we will be able to help. Once we get you up and running, you will be able to spend and skip payments knowing that your house will be taking care of the bill."

"Where have you guys been all this time? I really could have used your help a few years ago, but, hey, better late than never. Right?"

"That is correct."

"When will I receive the card?"

"We can send it out right away once we have entered all the information."

"How long will it take to get here?"

"That depends on how we send the card to you."

"So I have options?"

"Of course you do."

"Cool."

"So what is your full name?"

"Can you send the card by fax?"

"By fax?"

"Yes, by fax."

"No, that would only be a copy of the card."

"Oh, that's right."

"So your full name is?"

"Do you guys have access to a teleport machine?"

"A what?"

"A teleport machine?"

"I am pretty sure that they don't exist."

"I saw one on TV. They teleported a person."

"That was TV, not real." She paused. "So I have Ray. Is it Ray or Raymond?"

"How about carrier pigeon?"

"What?"

"Can you send the card by carrier pigeon?"

"That is not an option."

"Pony Express?"

"No."

"Dog sled team?"

"No."
"Nascar?"
"I think were done."
"Blue Angels?"
"Thank you."
"Paper airplane?...Blow tube?...Hot air balloon?"
All I heard was a click.

Solar Power

My cell phone rings. I answer, "Hello, this is Ray."

"This is Mark, and I am calling from International Solar. Have you heard about how installing solar panels can save you money?"

"No, I haven't." Who hasn't received a call from solar pusher?

"Well, Ray, this is your lucky day."

"I hope so. I just bought a lottery ticket for Wednesday's drawing, and the jackpot is over 400 million."

"The lottery is that high right now?"

"It is here in California. I've been trying to win for a long time, but they never call my name."

"I haven't won anything big."

"I haven't ever won anything in the Lottery. My wife told me that if I don't by a ticket, there's no way I can win. That kinda made sense to me."

"Yes, it does."

"I thought that they just called the names of people that lived in California. Sort of a 'yeah, you live here so you might win,' kinda thing."

"It does not work that way."

"I know that now, so I just spent $1 on a ticket hoping to win."

"So, about the solar program. We can make it so you don't have to pay for any power."

"Solar can run my entire home?"

"Yes it can."

"Do I have to convert any of my appliances?"

"No, not at all."

"Do I have to install any sort of converter?"

"Our panels connect directly into the grid."

"How do you do that?"

"We connect into the fuse panel."

"Will I have extra power available?"

"You could, depending on how much power you use."

"What do I do if I have extra power?"

"You would sell it back to the power company."

"I like that."

"It really is good for everyone."

"How many panels can I have?"

"That depends on the amount of power you need."

"Ok. How much do they cost?"

"That is the best part. They won't cost you anything out of pocket."

"Hmm. How does that work?"

"Well. The government has a program that allows qualified home owners to purchase these solar panels with their tax refunds over the next 5 years."

"What if my tax refund is only $5? Then $8, then $2, then $33, and then $6. Is the government going to keep my refunds of 5 plus 8 is 13…plus 2 is 15—"

"Ray, I was—"

"Wait you'll mess me up. Plus 33 is 43, 44, 45, 46, 47, 48 plus 6 is 49, 50, and 4, 54. So they will keep my $54 refund and give me the panels?"

"No, the cost of the panels is fixed. The government pays us for the panels and collects what they cost from you over the next five years."

"That's nice. You get paid right away, and I get to pay for them over the next five years with my tax refund. Is that right?"

"That is it in a nut shell."

"That sounds perfect. How much does each panel cost?"

"That depends on how many you need."

"How many panels would I need?"

"That depends on your power consumption."

"Ok. Let's say I need 30 panels."

"You won't need that many."

"25?"

"No, most people get fewer than 10 panels."

"So what would 10 panels cost me?"

"That would run about $32,000."

"What size home would that power?"

"Probably 5000 square feet."

"Oh! I might need *one* panel."

"You may, depending on your power consumption."

"How much is just one panel?"

"Over the five years, it works out to be only $2000 a year."

"That sounds good." What an idiot, I think, but I can keep him going for quite a while.

"Where do they put the panels?"

"We install them on the roof."

"What about the air conditioning unit?"

"If there's one in the way, we don't move it."

"So you install them around the unit?"

"If we need to."

"How heavy are they?"

"The technology has really come a long way. Each panel is only about twenty pounds."

"What are the dimensions of the panels?"

"They vary, depending on the configuration of the roof."

"My roof is flat."

"That is not a problem."

"Great."

"Shall we get started?"

"Sure."

"So, I need your full name."

"What about wind resistance?"

"What?"

"Wind resistance."

"That should be fine."

"Is there a maximum wind speed?"

"What do you mean?"

"Can they withstand, say, an 80 mph wind?"

"Yes, that won't be a problem. They are anchored to the roof."

"Oh, good."

"So is it Ray or Raymond?"

"These won't make the roof leak, right? I had a leak once, and it ruined the siding and carpet."

"Everything is patched and sealed. We guarantee no leaks."

"Wow, I am excited about solar now."

"So, Ray…"

"Will I lose any power going uphill?"

"I'm sorry?"

"Uphill."

"I'm not certain I understand, but as long as the sun is hitting the panels, they produce power."

"I love it." I shake my head. "Do I need to connect to any other power?"

"What do you mean?"

"Will I have power at night?"

"You will have power 24 hours a day. We don't change any of that."

"Nice."

"So I can get rid of the generator?"

"You have a generator?"

"Yes. When I don't have power, I use the generator."

"You can keep it if you want."

"Will I have the same horsepower?"

"Horsepower?"

"Yes, horsepower."

"I really don't understand now."

"I am converting my home to solar power, right?"

"Yes."

"So, I want to know if I will have the same horsepower."

"What do mean horsepower?"

"On my motorhome…."

"We cannot convert your motorhome to solar."

"Why not? You've convinced me, so I'm ready to go." I pause. "Hello…Hello…? I was just wondering how I sell the excess power back to the power company."

The line went dead.

The PACE Program

My cell phone rings, and I answer, "Hello, this is Ray."

"Hello, this is Brian, and I am calling from the Sacramento PACE program. Have you heard of us?"

"No, I haven't, but my uncle was a pace car driver. He drove a lot of different cars for some pretty big races. One time he was in an old fire engine—"

"No that is not the PACE program I am talking about."

"Oh, well, my niece used to be a runner and was responsible for the setting the pace for her college cross country track team. She could really run. She was—"

"No, it's not that kind of pace program either."

"Oh, my grandfather has a pace maker. It goes thump, thump, thump, click. Thump, thump, thump, click. It seems to us that that's probably not the right sound for a pace maker, but we're not doctors. Do you know if that is correct?"

"It does not sound like it to me, but I am not a doctor either. We are associated with Property Assessed Clean Energy."

"I see. Well we don't have a bidet. We were thinking about getting one to help the environment. You know save paper. We already live by, 'If it's yellow, leave it for next fellow, if it's brown, flush it down,' so getting a bidet would save paper, but we would use more water. That's the problem. Save a tree or save a fish. Can you see the dilemma?"

"What does PACE have to do with a bidet?"

"Properly Assed Clean Synergy. You know butt cleaning."

"No, it's Property Assessed Clean Energy. Air conditioners, windows, doors. We help with energy efficiency, renewable energy, or water efficiency projects. We provide special financing for those kinds of projects."

"Do you sell bidets? I've decided that I want to save trees…to help the spotted owls. I don't really like salmon, so trees get my vote."

"I'm sorry?"

"I like trees better than water."

"This has nothing to do with trees."

"Ok, I'll switch. I like water better than trees. Now can I get a bidet?"

"We don't sell bidets."

"What? Why are you wasting my time? I specifically called you to order a bidet."

"We called you."

"Mike, I called you. You said that I could get a bidet installed and that it would help save on my paper costs."

"This is Brian. I called you from the Sacramento PACE program."

"Is Mike there?"

"I don't know Mike."

"By talking to him I would think he's tall. I'd say 6' 1" or so, about 225 pounds, thinning brown hair, mid 60s maybe 63, 64."

"There is no Mike here."

"Where did he go? Do you expect him back soon?"

"Mike does not work here."

"What? He was an excellent salesman. Did he do something wrong? I always thought he sounded a bit suspicious."

"Mike has never worked in this office."

"Can you transfer me to the other office?"

"There is not another office."

"I thought this was a big operation."

"This is a program that is offered to home owners in California."

"I see. Well, it seems we have a couple of problems here."

"What are the problems?"

"Well you made me switch to water from trees, and I want to switch back. I really like trees."

"That is not my problem."

"And now you've somehow lost Mike. He was a good friend."

"I don't know any Mike."

"On top of all that, I still want a bidet."

"I'm sorry, but I can't help you there."

"Finally, I do not own a home." All I heard was a click.

Police Officers Association

My cell phone rings and I answer it, "Hello this is Ray."

"Good evening. This is Officer Campbell, and I am calling on behalf of all the fallen officers. How are you?"

"I could be better. I have a little bit of a cough and some phlegm that occasionally comes up when I cough hard. My left side hurts when I bend to the right, my right cheek is swollen from a tooth extraction earlier today, and my dog decided that he really liked my couch, so he ate it. Other than that, today has been really good."

"I am sorry to hear about all the aches and pains and your dog."

"Thanks. Yesterday, my son wrecked both my cars He was driving too fast coming home, slid around the corner, lost control, and smashed into my other car. Two for one kinda. Except in the opposite direction. All bad."

"Wow. Sorry to hear about that."

"Were you on the call?"

"What?"

"There were a lot of police out here yesterday. Were you one of them?"

"I'm sorry, I was not. I am calling from Nashville."

"Nashville? Have you ever been to Graceland? I hear it is pretty awesome."

"Graceland is a nice place to visit, however it is in Memphis."

"Oh yeah. That's right." I burst out into song. "We're going to Graceland, Graceland, in Memphis, Tennessee. I'm going to Graceland."

"Paul Simon, love it."

"Me, too. I sing a lot of karaoke. That's one I really like."

"Very nice. So, I am calling for a program that helps the families of fallen officers."

"Do you know Ken Richards?"

"Ken Richards?"

"Yes, he was a police officer that used to teach water skiing at a youth camp I sent my children to. He was always explaining to the kids that if you fall, get right back up and try again. He used to fall a lot."

"No, this program is for the families of fallen officers."

"I see. All right, I want to help. Is it going to be in Nashville? What is the theme? If possible can I sing or act? I can be support back stage if needed, but I like to be in front of people."

"That is not the kind of program I am talking about."

"Oh. It's a paper thing. I can't draw very well, but I am willing to try my best."

"What we are asking for is money to help support the families of fallen officers."

"Why do they need more money?"

"To help offset the cost of the surviving in today's economy."

"If I send you $10 to help them, how will it be replaced to help *me* in today's economy?"

"We are providing a better service for our community because of the money sent by concerned citizens like yourself."

"I thought that the money was for the families."

"It *is* for the families."

"Are those families the ones helping out in the community?"

"I don't understand."

"You said that the money is going to help the families of fallen officers, right?"

"That is correct."

"Ok, so if a child gets knocked down by a dog in the park around the corner from my house, the $10 I send to Nashville to help one of the families of the fallen officers will pay for that family to come out and deal with the dog?"

"No, not one of the families, one of the officers in your town would come and deal with the dog."

"So did my $10 pay him to help my community here?"

"Not really. The money you send is to help the families of fallen officers."

"Oh, what about the dog in the park?"

"What about the dog?"

"What happened to it?"

"What happened to the dog?"

"Yes, where is it now?"

"I don't know."

"What do you mean you don't know? What do you do with dogs that are picked up at a park?"

"We usually take them to the animal shelter."

"Do you know when the dog can be adopted?"

"What?"

"I want a different dog. One that doesn't eat couches."

"There wasn't a dog."

"Yes, there was. Remember the dog that knocked down a child in the park and was taken to the animal shelter…how long before that dog can be adopted?"

"Three weeks."

"Nice, I can't wait. I'm going to call him… Do you know if it was a male or female dog?"

"No, I don't know."

"Pat, I'm going to call the dog Pat."

"Ok."

"So, the $10 you want to send to us—"

"Is all the money sent to you for the families of fallen officers used here?"

"Almost."

"What do you mean almost?"

"The money is divide up between all states."

"So I really need to send more money to you, say $50."

"That would be super."

"I'm still trying to figure out the best way to help support my community. Let me get this straight…if I send $50 and it gets divided among all the states. Are all the states equal?"

"Yes."

"Even if we have more fallen officer families?"

"Yes, it is split evenly."

"Ok, so $50 divided by 50 states is $1 per state. I live in California, so will my money be divided evenly into California?"

"Yes, each state receives money that they then distribute among the cities."

"Got it. So, the 2010 Census shows that there 482 cities in California. My dollar split among them would be about $1/5^{th}$ of cent. Sounds as if I need to send even more money."

"Yes, you do. In order for your town to see any significant funding we would need a large contribution from you."

"I can see that. So if I sent you 10 times as much…$500…my town would see 10 times that $1/5^{th}$ a cent, or 2 cents."

"Yes."

"So $5000 will get us $0.20 and $50,000 will get $2?"

"You are doing the math correct."

"Wow. That is a lot of money for my town."

"Well, there are a lot of fallen officer families."

"So if I understand this correctly. I should sell everything I own, max out all my credit cards and borrow the rest to send $50,000 to you, so that my town will get $2…and a 6 person homeless family collecting welfare and sponging off the system. Is that correct?"

"No, you can still work. We would not want you to quit working to collect welfare. That shouldn't be the only income for you and your family."

"Oh, that makes sense. So, I'm homeless, working with no place to live, no cars because of my son, my dog will be healthier because he won't be eating the couch, and I won't have any bills, because I have no home. Does that about cover it?"

"There are shelters available."

"That's an incredible idea. Do you know if I can bring a dog to the shelter?"

"I would assume you could."

"This plan might work. How exciting. Ruin my life so I can send money to someone I don't know in Nashville."

"I never said ruin your life."

"Can I write a check?"

"We can do a wire transfer."

"Really? A wire transfer? Do you actually think I'm going to send you money?"

"I was hoping."

"Do you believe in the tooth fairy, too?"

All I heard was a click.

ASPCA

My cell phone rings and I answer it, "Hello, this is Ray."

"Hello, this is Scott. I am calling from The American Society for the Prevention of Cruelty to Animals or ASPCA. We are seeking donations for the care of many animals. Do you think that you and your family might be able to help out?"

"Who is this?"

"My name is Scott."

"Hi, Scott."

"Hello."

"Where are you calling from?"

"I am calling from The American Society for the Prevention of Cruelty to Animals or ASPCA."

"I see, well not actually *see*, but I hear what you're saying. You're Scott, and you're calling from the American Society for the prevention…."

"Of cruelty to animals."

"Ok, so where are you calling from?"

"Like I just said, I'm calling from The American Society for the Prevention of Cruelty to Animals or ASPCA."

"I totally understand that part…ASPCA. I want to know your location."

"I am located in India."

"India?" This call make take a while. He called the wrong guy, and I have a lot of questions…irrelevant questions, of course.

"Yes, we are contracted by the ASPCA to make phone calls to try to solicit donations for animal shelters."

"Wow. What is the weather like over in India right now?"

"It is warm. I would say 26 or 27."

"So what is that in Fahrenheit?"

"About 80 degrees."

"Do you get a lot of rain?"

"Not much."

"Wind?"

"Yes we have quite a bit of wind."
"What about sand?"
"What about the sand?"
"Do you have a lot of sand?"
"This is India. Of course we have a lot of sand."
"Is there a water shortage?"
"We are always in some sort of drought."
"Do you have grass?"
"What do you mean?"
"Do you have a lawn at your house?"
"I do."
"What kind of grass is it?"
"I don't know. It's grass."
"Is it a fescue, Kentucky bluegrass, ryegrass, creeping bentgrass, Bermuda?"
"I'm not sure."
"I'll bet it is a Bermuda. Bermuda is really drought tolerant, and being in India…well you know."
"Ok."
"Do you have any pets?"
"We have a dog."
"So do I."
"What kind of dog do you have?"
"It is just a mutt."
"Mine, too. They seem to make the best dogs."
"So, we are trying to get funding for animal rescue projects."
"Do you have a camel?"
"What?"
"Do you own a camel?"
"No, I have a car."
"I heard that most people in India own camels."
"I don't own a camel."
"Do any of your neighbors have camels?"
"No."
"Did you have a camel growing up?"

"No, I grew up in the city."

"In the city? Do they have camel parking lots? You know for the people that drive camels to work."

"No. Most people drive cars."

"What about all the camels?"

"What about them?"

"Where are they?"

"I don't know."

"You *do* have camels in India, right?"

"We do."

"Hmm. What kind of car do you have?"

"I own a Ford Taurus."

"Fix or repair daily."

"What?"

"Ford, fix or repair daily."

"I don't understand."

"That is what Ford means. F.O.R.D. Fix or repair daily."

"Oh, I haven't had any problems with my car."

"I have a Toyota pickup. Love it."

"So can we count on you for a donation to—?"

"Have you ever eaten camel?"

"I have."

"I hear it tastes like chicken."

"It tastes like a cross between lamb and beef."

"That sound yummy. I really like lamb. And how can you go wrong with beef?"

"The shelters are depending on donations from—"

"What about the hump?"

"The hump?"

"Yes, does it taste different?"

"No, it tastes like camel."

"What about chickens?"

"What about them?"

"Do you have chickens?"

"No."

"There aren't any chickens in India?"

"There are chickens in India. I just don't own any chickens."

"Oh. Do you know what the temperature for baby chickens should be?"

"I am not sure."

"I was thinking somewhere around 180."

"I think that might be too hot."

"What about salmonella?"

"I'm sorry?"

"Salmonella."

"What about it?"

"Aren't you supposed to get rid of Salmonella with high temperatures?"

"I don't think it goes away like that."

"Can't you get Salmonella from undercooked chicken?"

"I believe you can."

"So 180 would be the correct temperature for the chicks."

"No, not 180."

"Why not?"

"It is way too high."

"All the books say 180."

"Not for chicks."

"Only the adult chickens?"

"No, 180 is still too high. That would make them crispy."

"Right. I'm making chick pops. Crispy Chick Pops."

"Are you kidding me?"

"Have you ever had balut?"

"That is the chicken egg thing, right?"

"Yes, it's gross. The completely other end of the spectrum. Baby chicks, deep fried to perfection, so they can be dipped into your favorite sauces. Ranch is the best, some like Thousand Island dressing or honey mustard."

All I heard was a click.

National Auto Insurance

My cell phone rings, "Hello, this is Ray."
"Good morning."
"Good morning."
"This is Margret, and I am calling from National Auto. I wanted to let you that right now the rates for auto insurance have gone down drastically."
"Good morning."
"Good morning."
"Who is this?"
"This is Margret."
"Margret who?"
"Margret Anderson."
"Margret Anderson?"
"Yes."
"Good morning."
"Good morning."
"How can I help you?"
"I am calling to let you know that the rates for auto insurance have gone down drastically."
"How far down have they gone?"
"Insurance rates have gone down drastically."
"How far is drastically?"
"Drastically is just a term we use to say that they have come down a lot."
"How far is a lot?"
"It really depends on the car you drive and your driving record."
"So if my car is a 1984 VW Rabbit and I had a perfect driving record, would I have the lowest rates possible?"
"That is a possibility."
"What if it were a 1995 Ford Ranger 4X4?"
"Is that the car you currently own?"
"No."

"What type car do you currently drive?"
"I have a couple of cars."
"What car do you drive the most?"
"What do you mean by 'the most'?"
"Which car do you drive more?"
"What do you mean 'more'?"
"Which car do you drive the most during the week?"
"Drive to where?"
"Drive to work."
"Which job?"
"How many jobs do you have?"
"I have 3 jobs."
"Do you drive for a living?"
"No."
"Do you drive the same car all week?"
"No."
"Which car do you drive the most?"
"For what?"
"Your job."
"Which job?"
"What do you do for a living?"
"I work as a telemarketer. I'm a greeter at Walmart," I pause, "Good morning," I pause again, Good morning," then I continue, "and I work as a caregiver."
"Do you drive to work?"
"Which job?"
"Do you drive to work for all your jobs?"
"Yes."
"How many miles is it to your place of employment?"
"Which place?"
"Which ever job is the farthest away."
"Farthest away?"
"The farthest from your home."

"My caregiver job is 2 miles away from my home, and my Walmart and telemarketing jobs are both 1.5 miles away but in different directions."

"How many miles do you drive each week?"

"For my job?"

"Yes."

"Which job?"

"How many miles do you drive for all your jobs?"

"Each week?"

"Yes."

"I drive maybe 30 miles each week for my jobs."

"Only 30 miles for all your jobs?"

"Well, let me see, 1.5 miles to my telemarketing job on Mondays, and back home is another 1.5 miles. That makes 3 miles so far. Usually on Mondays I go help Mike with his lunch. Mike is 2 miles away from my house and 1 mile from Walmart. After lunch I go to work at Walmart. When I get off at Walmart I head home, 1.5 miles. So on Mondays I drive 7.5 miles for work."

"So about 7.5 miles a day."

"No. I don't work the telemarketing on Tuesday or Thursday. On Tuesday I work at Walmart in the morning and have lunch with Mike, then back to Walmart, and then home again. So 1.5 plus 1 is 2.5, plus 1, then 3.5 plus 1.5, so 5 miles on Tuesday."

"Tuesday and Thursday is 5 miles each day?"

"No. I don't work at Walmart on Thursday."

"How about Wednesday?"

"On Wednesday I go to my telemarketing job, 1.5 miles and then I go to Walmart. Walmart is 2.5 miles from my telemarketing job, so on Wednesday I drive 1.5 miles plus 2.5 miles which is 4 miles, then home 1.5 miles. I don't see Mike on Wednesdays, so on Wednesday I drive 5.5 miles."

"Ok, we can say 25 miles a week."

"Well, On Thursday I only have lunch with Mike. So that would be 4 miles."

"So 25 sounds good."

81

"Not really. On Friday I work at my telemarketing job, come home, then I have lunch with Mike. So that would be 1.5 plus 1.5 makes 3, plus the 4 miles for Mike, so 7 miles on Friday for work."

"That sounds more like 30 miles for work each week."

"I added it up and came out with 29 miles. Let me check, On Monday I drive 1.5 to my tele—"

"Close enough…29 is good."

"Ok."

"So you drive 29 miles a week."

"For my jobs?"

"Yes for your jobs."

"Yes."

"So we can say that you probably drive around 125 miles a month."

"No."

"Those are the numbers you gave me."

"Yes for my job."

"Do you drive more?"

"Of course."

"Where else are you driving?"

"On Friday after lunch with Mike, I might drive over to the coast or into the mountains or out to the desert to go camping."

"Do you do that every weekend?"

"Mostly."

"What do you drive?"

"When?"

"On the weekend."

"Where?"

"When you go camping."

"Where?"

"To the coast."

"I usually take my car to the coast. We stay at the Hyatt and then UBER around and look at different homes."

"What kind of car is it you drive to the coast?"

"It's a 2014 Ford Fusion."

"Is that the same car you drive to the mountains?"

"No."

"What car do you drive to the mountains?"

"That would be a 2017 Thor Four Winds Siesta 24SR Motorhome."

"Ok, so what car do you drive to the desert?"

"I drive my 1976 Jeep."

"How many miles do you think you drive each month?"

"To where?"

"Total."

"What?"

"What is the total amount of miles you might drive each month?"

"Which month?"

"What?"

"Well we tend to go to the coast every month, either the first or second weekend of each month. During the colder months we go to the desert and the hotter months we go to the mountains."

"How many miles is the coast trip?"

"It's 226 miles round trip."

"How far are the mountains?"

"About 400 miles round trip."

"How about the desert?"

"About the same, 400 miles, maybe a little more…say 410 miles."

"Do you go to the coast more than one weekend a month?"

"No only once a month."

"So you probably drive really close to the same amount each month since the mountains and desert are the same distance for your home."

"No. The desert is a little farther."

"Ok, can we assume that you drive for your job and weekend adventures somewhere between 2000 and 2500 miles per month?"

"I think it is less than that. 125 miles during the week times 4.3, plus—"

"What do you think the total number of miles you drive each month for your job and your weekend adventures might be?"

"I would say 1550 miles is closer to the actual miles for those activities."

"So you drive 1550 miles a month?"

"No."

"No."

"No, during the week I might go to the store, out to dinner, to the movies. You know just living stuff."

"How many miles do you drive for those activities?"

"Maybe 150 miles a week."

"So an additional about 645 miles a month?"

"That sounds right."

"It looks like you drive somewhere between 2000 and 2500 miles a month?"

"For everything…yes."

"That's what I said earlier."

"No you said for my jobs and weekend adventures it might be between 2000 and 2500. That was not right."

"I'm sorry. My bad."

"What?"

"It was my mistake. I'm sorry."

"Mistake? What mistake? Is my math wrong?"

"No, everything is great. I am assuming that you drive the Ford or Jeep to work. Is that correct?"

"Depends on which day."

"But it is one of those cars, correct?"

"Yes."

"Great. Let's move on. How is your driving record?"

"Not so good."

"How bad is it?"

"Well, I expect to get my license back in 3 years."

All I heard was a click.

World Wide Vacations

My cell phone rings, "Hello, this is Ray."

"Good afternoon, this is Beth, and I am calling from World Wide Vacations. Have you ever heard of us?"

"I have not."

"Well we are a company that specializes in vacation rentals all over the world."

"That is nice."

"Are you married?"

"I am."

"How long have you been married?"

"Which time?"

"Which time?"

"Yes, which wife are you talking about?"

"How many are there?"

"Currently there is just one wife. Legally you can't be married to more than one woman at a time."

"I mean how many times have you been married?"

Here we go. This is going to be fun. "If I count the woman I married in the Philippians, that the Navy said wasn't real, 8 times.""

"You have been married 8 times."

"Actually, 9 times. There was Natalie in Mexico."

"Wow."

"Wow?"

"I have never met someone married so many times."

"I like being married."

"I can see that."

"Did you take a lot of vacations?"

"I did. I took a lot of vacations. That is where I met most of my wives."

"Do you still take vacations?"

"No."

"Why not."

"I married now. I only travel when I am searching for a new wife."

"Have you ever traveled *with* your wife?"

"No. Why would I do that?"

"To share the experiences."

"Hmmm, I guess some people do that."

"Yes, that is why most people take vacations."

"Not to look for new spouses?"

"No, they travel to share the experience and discover new and exciting places."

"But it is so expensive to travel with 2 people."

"That is where we can help you out."

"Tell me how." Have I got some questions for her.

"Ray, here at World Wide Vacations, we have contracted with the top resorts around the world to use their surplus inventory."

"What do you mean?"

"When a resort has rooms that are not booked at times, they would rather fill them at a lower rate than have the rooms empty."

"Why would they do that?"

"They are paying staff regardless if the room is filled or not."

"I see, so I can get rooms super cheap."

"You can get them at about 75% off the normal rack rate."

"That sounds pretty nice."

"Yes, it is an amazing offer."

"What do I have to do?"

"We sell memberships to this club that allows you to purchase these trips and at very discounted rates."

"Where can I go?"

"Anywhere in the world."

"Like where?"

"Where would you like to go, Ray?"

"I've never been to Kansas."

"Kansas?"

"I love the Wizard of Oz and have always wanted to see Kansas."

"You can go anywhere in the world and you have chosen Kansas?"

"That's not a good choice?"

"It is a fine choice."

"What do have available in Murdock, Kansas?"

"Murdock, Kansas?"

"Yes."

"Why there?"

"I really liked the movie Airplane and the pilot's name was Murdock."

"I see. Let me look."

"Did you know that population of Murdock was 219 people in 2016?"

"We won't have anything close to Murdock, Kansas."

"Oh."

"How about somewhere outside the United States?"

"Ok. Alaska."

"Alaska?"

"Sure. It's outside the US."

"Not really."

"Sure it is."

"No. It is not outside the US."

"Yes it is. Do you own a home?"

"Yes."

"Do you have children?"

"Yes."

"Do they have bicycles?"

"Yes."

"Do you own them or are they rented?"

"We own them."

"Are they inside your home or outside home?"

"They are outside."

"Just like Alaska."

"But Alaska is part of the US."

"Yes, but it's outside the US."

"Alaska is one of the 50 states, so it is *in* the US."
"Ohhhh. That makes sense now. Hawaii is outside?"
"No, it is same thing."
"I see."
"What about Washington DC?"
"That is in the US."
"But, it's not a state."
"That's true that it's not a state, but it is still in the US."
"How about Canada?"
"We have resorts all over Canada. Do you want to go to Canada?"
"No, How about Europe?"
"Certainly, where in Europe do you want to go?"
"I don't have a clue."
"Would you like to go to Sweden?"
"Nope."
"How about Wales?"
"No."
"Greece?"
"No."
"Germany."
"Germany is in Europe?"
"Yes. It is considered part of Europe."
"No, not Germany."
"Italy, Portugal, Ireland, Scotland, Spain?"
"No. What about Finland?"
"We have resorts in Finland. Would you like to go to Finland?"
"Not really. How about Hungry?"
"Yes, we have quite a few resorts in Hungry. Shall we look at some of those?"
"No. What about Turkey?"
"Yes. Do you want to go there?"
"No.
"What about Mexico?"

"We have resorts all over Mexico. Do you have any place in mind?"

"How about Puerto Vallarta?"

"We have about 20 properties in Puerto Vallarta. Do you want to go to Puerto Vallarta?"

"No, my ex-wife lives there. Her dad doesn't really like me that much."

"Ray, I really just need a place you would like to visit."

"I'm still set on Murdock, Kansas."

"We don't have any resorts there."

"Not even a Hyatt?"

"Not there."

"A Days Inn?"

"No."

"How about a Motel 6?"

"Ray, are you interested in planning and taking a vacation or not?"

"Well, my wife isn't really that good of a cook, and I have been married almost 4 years, so if I were to file for divorce, it would be 6 months before it would be finalized, so I could be ready to travel in about 7 months. How about if you call me then."

"That won't work. This plan is for right now."

"Are *you* single, Beth? *Could* you be single in 7 months?"

All I heard was a click.

Federal Grant Program

I'm on my way to the store, and my cellphone rings. My car connects the call and I say, "Hello. This is Ray."

"Good afternoon. This is David, and I am calling from the Federal Grant Program. You have been selected as a candidate for a once in a lifetime program opportunity."

"I have?"

"Yes, we called you because of your credit score and outstanding history with the IRS."

"Wow." I know my credit isn't that good, and I don't know anyone who has an "outstanding history" with the IRS, but I continue, "Tell me more I'm very interested."

"Again my name is David, and I called you to let you know that we have $8500 waiting for you in the form of a federal grant."

"That's great."

"It is, and this money is not a loan. It does not need to be paid back…ever. It does not even need to be reported as income. It is free money. This is money that you can keep and use in whatever fashion you like."

"I don't like fashion."

"I don't mean fashion like clothes. I mean you can use it however you would like, so what would you do with $8500, Ray?"

"I'm not sure. That's a nice chunk of change. What would you do?"

"Well, I would probably take a vacation with my family."

"That sounds nice. How many are in your family, David?"

"I am married and have 3 children."

"Wonderful. What are the ages of your children?"

"My oldest is 17, a son, then I have two daughters 15 and 10."

"I'm thinking that a Disney vacation would be perfect for you, David."

"We have done the Disney thing. My kids loved it."

"David, have you ever taken your family on a cruise?"

"No. My wife is afraid of the ocean."

"I can see how that would make a cruise out of the question."
"Yes, it would."
"David, have you considered about travel overseas?"
"We thought about that, but that can be expensive."
"It can be, but if you applied for this federal grant of $8500 like you want me to do, maybe we can go together."
"I am not allowed to apply for this grant."
"Why not?"
"As an employee of the program, I am ineligible."
"That sucks."
"It does, so are you married?"
"I am."
"Do you have any children?"
"I do."
"Do they live with you?"
"No. They are older and have their own families."
"So this money would just be for you and your wife?"
"I have to share it?"
"Ummm, no, you don't have to, but if you want to share it…I guess…I just assumed that you would tell her."
"Yes, I probably would tell her."
"Good."
"Why is that good?"
"I don't know. I just figured…."
"Just figured what?"
"I didn't figure anything."
"You said that you just figured."
"I did. It was my mistake."
"What was the mistake?"
"I don't know."
"You said that you made a mistake."
"I guess I assumed that you would tell your wife about the money."
"David, you should never make those assumptions."
"I shouldn't."

"I may not have told my wife about the money. I might have used the money to pay for my girlfriend's apartment. I might have bought some drugs. Maybe gone to the casino and gambled it away. There are so many things I could have done with the money that did not involve my wife."

"That is true. I am sorry."

"Don't be sorry. Just don't do it again."

"Not a problem. Again, I'm sorry."

"You are forgiven."

"So, Ray, what would you do with the money?"

"I'm not sure. What would you do again?"

"I would take a vacation."

"Where would you go?"

"I haven't been to Europe, so maybe there."

"Do you know what country?"

"Maybe Spain."

"Why Spain?"

"That's the only one I could think of."

"That makes perfect sense…go to Spain because I can say 'Spain.'"

"Maybe I would run with the bulls."

"That's stupid."

"What?"

"Have you seen how many people get trampled by those bulls?"

"Yes."

"So you want to go to Spain, get trampled by bulls, and end up in traction in a foreign hospital while on vacation?"

"I guess not."

"Don't run with the bulls, David. Just visit Spain."

"That makes sense. What would you do, Ray?"

"There are so many things that I could do."

"Like what?"

I finally arrive at the store, switch the call to my Bluetooth earpiece, and head in to do my shopping. "Well, my fence really needs some repairs, there is a leak in the bathroom sink, and my dishwasher needs to be replaced."

"So you want to do some repairs around the house?"

"Not really, those are things that need to be done, but I don't want to do them."

"I see, is there anything else?"

"Around the house, oh, yes. There is the—"

"No, I mean is there anything else that you might want to do with the money?"

"I'd really like to get a 75" LED TV."

"That sounds like a plan."

"Not really."

"No?"

"I don't have the room for it. I just want one."

"Ok. Anything else?"

"A new car maybe."

"A new car?"

"Sure."

"I don't think you can buy a new car for $8500."

"I could use the money as a down payment."

"You certainly could. Is that what you want to do?"

"Nope."

"What do you think you want to do?"

"I don't know. Maybe a vacation, like you said."

"That sounds like a great idea. Where would you go?"

"I don't know. Maybe a trip to Spain to see the people running with the bulls get trampled."

"Ha, ha. That's what I said, too."

"I know, I couldn't think of any place for a vacation either."

"Is that what you want to do the most?"

"Nope."

"So, I can see that you are undecided with what to do with the money, Ray, but this is free money and you can do whatever you would like to do."

"How do I get the money?"

"We have three options for you. We can send the money to a credit or debit card, or we can put the money directly into a checking or savings account, or you can pick it up at a Western Union or Money Gram. Are any of those good for you?"

"Yes, they all are."

"Which one would you like to use."

"I don't care."

"Ok, why don't we send the money to a credit or debit card?"

"Perfect."

"Which card would you like to use."

"It doesn't matter to me. One with a low interest rate. And maybe airline miles. I might be taking a trip in the near future."

"Sounds good. Which card?"

"How about American Airlines...wait their leg room is terrible. US airways seem to be good, but they don't fly as far. Oh, oh, oh, I know. United Airlines. I want a United Airlines card."

"Ok, let's use that one."

"Which one?"

"Your United Airlines card."

"I don't have one."

"If we are going to send money to a credit card, you need to have that card."

"Oh, I don't have any credit cards. I thought you were going to give me one."

"Why don't we send the money to a bank account?"

"Perfect."

"Where would you like us to send the money?"

"The closest bank is Wells Fargo."

"Ok, what is your account number there?"

"I don't have an account there."

"You need to have an account at a bank or credit union for us to send money there. Do you have an account at a bank or credit union?"

"No."

"So I guess we'll need to send the money by Western Union or Money Gram, right?"

"Perfect."

"Are you close to a Walmart or Walgreens?"

"Walmart," I tell him truthfully. There's a Walmart right across the parking lot from where I'm shopping right now.

"How far away are you from Walmart?"

"About 20 minutes." If I walk…slowly.

"When can you go to Walmart?"

"I can leave right now."

"Ok, start heading to Walmart, and I will fill in all the info for the grant."

"I'm driving as we speak," I say as I toss a box of cereal into my cart.

"Are you heading to Walmart?"

"I am."

"Great. First off I need your address."

"I'm between homes right now."

"What do you mean?"

"I live in my camper."

"Do you have a permanent address?"

"I did, but I don't now."

"Ok, we can still work with that. What city are you in?"

"Sacramento, Ca."

"What is the zip code?"

"95826."

"Ok, we already have your cell number, so when you get to Walmart, I am going to need you to call our verification line and give them this number. Do you have a pen and some paper?"

"I do."

"The verification code is TG207."

"TG207," I repeat back to him.

"Yes. The authorization code is 451-458-4551-CBC."

"451-458-4551-CVC," I say.

"No. CBC"

"Yes, I got that. CVC."

"No, Charlie, Bob, Charlie."

"Oh! CBC. Ok."

"The number you need to call is (727) 324-6231, and our authenticator will assist you with the transaction." [That's the real number! Give them a call if you want. See if they'll give you a federal grant.]

"Ok, David, will do."

"Call us when you get to Walmart."

"As soon as I get there. Thanks."

I finish my shopping and stop at the food court to get a hot dog and drink for lunch. About 20 minutes later I get another call. "Hello. This is Ray."

"Hello, this is James, and I am the authenticator for the Federal Grant Program. Have you made it to Walmart?"

"I have. I'm just walking inside."

"Great. So let me reiterate the program. The $8500 that you will be receiving is a federal grant. It is money that does not need to be paid back. It can be used for anything that your heart desires, but there are some rules that need to be followed because you live in California."

"What are the rules?"

"In order for the transaction to be legal there needs to be a transaction between you and the program."

"Like what?"

"You will need to establish an account with our program. Once the account is established, we will put the money into that account, and it can be withdrawn from Walmart Money Gram."

"How do I open an account?"

"Walmart has Apple Cards that you can purchase."

"Yes."

"Purchase two Apple Cards and go to the Money Gram counter. I will stay on the phone with you."

"Ok." I'm sitting in the food court watching a basketball game, but I create a fake conversation for James to overhear.

"I like to purchase these Apple Cards."

Putting my hand over the microphone to muffle the sound, I say, "Apples? What apples. Where are they?"

Hand off. "I just need the cards from the apples."

Hand on. "We don't sell just the tags, you need to buy the whole bag of apples."

Hand off. "Hold on." I pause. "James?"

"Yes, Ray?"

"They aren't letting me buy the apple tags."

"Ray, you need Apple Cards."

"These are the cards from the apples. I grabbed two Golden Delicious cards."

"No, Ray. Apple Cards are like credit cards."

"What?"

"They are gift cards. You need to purchase two $100 Apple Cards. Can you do that?"

"No."

"What is the problem?"

"I don't have $200."

"Call us when you do." Then just a click.

US Mortuary

My cell phone rings. I answer, "Hello, this is Ray."

"Good morning."

"Good morning."

"My name is Terry, and I am calling from US Mortuary Coverage. Have you heard of us?"

"No."

"We provide families the opportunity to obtain insurance to help cover the cost of funeral services."

"I see. Tell me more."

"Did you know that the average cost for a funeral can be in the range of $10,000?"

"No, I didn't know that."

"Sometimes it can be much higher than that."

"How so?"

"Depending on the services you may want."

"Like what?"

"It would depend on the package you request."

"Give me an example."

"Well there is the cost for the mortuary, embalming, the casket, the service itself, the hall rental, the reception after the service, the flowers, a head stone. As you can see there are many costs associated with the loss of a family member."

"Oh, my. I never really thought about any of that."

"That is why we are calling, Ray. To help families set aside some money to help offset the cost of a funeral."

"What about cremation, Terry?"

"What about it?"

"Is it more?"

"I don't think so."

"I mean all the fuel used to incinerate the body, who has to pay for that?"

"That would be included in the cost from the mortuary."

"They don't break it down?"

"No."

"It would be a whole lot less fuel for an infant than a 500 pound man."

"True."

"So the infant should be cheaper, right?"

"I would assume so, but that is all decided by the mortuary."

"What if someone dies while they are traveling outside the country?"

"We have Outside US supplemental insurance available to purchase to protect the family if that were to happen."

"Hmm. Does it matter where they are when they die?"

"What do you mean?"

"Let's say they die in Victoria, British Columbia, would the insurance be the same for someone who died in say Suva, Fiji?"

"Yes, the Outside US supplemental insurance that is purchased would cover deaths out of the country."

"Any country?"

"Yes."

"Does it matter if it is an infant or 500 pound man?"

"No."

"So the Outside US supplemental insurance is for the transportation of the deceased body?"

"Yes."

"To where?"

"To their home town."

"What if we want to have the service held in a different town?"

"We also have available for purchase a Change of Venue supplemental insurance."

"What does that cover?"

"If for some reason the deceased person's family needs to have the service in a different location, then that can be a covered expense."

"I don't understand."

"So, Ray, let's say that maybe they lived in California and had a family plot in Kentucky. This Change of Venue supplemental insurance would cover that expense."

"Nice. Would it matter if it were an infant or 500 pound man?"

"No, not at all."

"What about the other family members?"

"What about them?"

"Does this insurance cover the cost of travel back from Suva, Fiji, for the family that now has to cut their vacation short because of the death?"

"The Outside US supplemental insurance does not cover that."

"Do you have an insurance to cover that?"

"Actually, we do. We have an Accidental Death of Family Member supplemental insurance."

"What does that cover?"

"This insurance will pay for the transportation of all members of the immediate family that were on vacation with the deceased."

"Transportation where?"

"Back to the originating airport."

"What about the hotel expense?"

"What about it?"

"What if we were there on vacation for two weeks, and a family member dies on the third day. Do we have to pay for the rest of the hotel stay or can we get a refund?"

"That depends."

"Depends on what?"

"If it was a package that was purchased from a tour company, you may be able to get some sort of refund if you purchased travel insurance from them."

"What if it wasn't a package?"

"The hotel might refund the unused portion of your stay, but that would be up to the hotel."

"Do you have any insurance to cover that?"

"We do not have a supplemental insurance to cover that."

"What about excursions that were planned on the vacation?"

"You probably would need to check with those separately."

"No supplemental to cover those?"

"I'm sorry, we cannot cover everything."

"A family could sure lose a lot of money if someone dies while on vacation."

"They surely could. That's why we here at US Mortuary are in business."

"So that people die?"

"No, no, no. We are in business to help offset the cost of funeral expenses when a family member passes."

"What kind of passing?"

"I'm sorry?"

"Does it matter how they died?"

"What do you mean?"

"What if they die in an airplane crash?"

"They are covered."

"Car crash?"

"Covered, as long as it wasn't alcohol or drug related."

"What if it was the other driver that was intoxicated?"

"Then that would be a covered event."

"What if they were driving an electric car, and it started to rain real bad, and there was a short in the car, and they get electrocuted."

"That would be covered. Basically we cover anything that can be considered an uncontrolled death. An accident that is out of their control."

"What about sports?"

"Sports accidents are covered."

"So does the insurance cover sky diving, bungee jumping, and wing suit flying?"

"Actually, it does not cover those activities."

"Why?"

"Because you would be putting yourself in a controlled accident."

"I don't get it?"

"You have the choice to bungee jump or sky dive. If you die, that was your choice."

"I see."

"Do you do any of those?"

"No way. Too scary." I pause. "What about murder?"

"Again, we cover anything that can be considered an uncontrolled death, so murder would be covered."

"I'm guessing that suicide would not be covered."

"That is correct. It would be considered controlled death."

"I see that."

"So, Ray, as you can see we have a lot of options available."

"You sure do."

"If you purchase a basic plan from US Mortuary, you may add as many supplemental insurances you would like. "

"Terry, does the size of a person that died play into the cost?"

"No, our cost is based on the age of the family members on the covered plan."

"Based on age?"

"Yes."

"How do you determine that cost?"

"How many family members do you have?"

"It is just me."

"Are you married?"

"No."

"Do you have any children?"

"No."

"Any siblings?"

"No."

"Are your parents alive?"

"No."

"So the insurance you would be purchasing would be for yourself."

"Yes."

"How old are you Ray?"

"I am 50."

"Would you be interested in any of the supplemental insurances?"

"Not really, those are to help get the family members back to the US and a change of venue. Since I don't have any family members to get back and I don't have a different venue, I won't need those supplemental insurances. "

"Well, Ray, the basic plan based on your age of 50 is only $257.40 a year which breaks down to only $4.95 a week."

"Is there another plan?"

"Of course, we have a Plus, Premium, and Platinum Plan."

"What is the difference?"

"The basic plan is for $10,000 in coverage. The Plus is $20,000, the Premium $40,000, and the Platinum is $80,000."

"What is the weekly breakdown of the cost?"

"Starts at $4.95, then $7.95, $15.95, and finally $29.95 for the Platinum."

"I like the Premium plan."

"Great, let's get you signed up."

"Alright."

"What is your full name?"

"It's Ray… Who gets the money when I die?"

"You can leave it to any family member you like."

"I don't have any family, remember?"

"Right, you can leave the money to an organization."

"Which one?"

"Any one you like."

"Have you ever heard of the program that helps fallen officers?"

"No."

"It's a program in Nashville, TN, that will send money to help the families of fallen officers. The money is divide up between all cities in all the states. They told me that the best way to help support my community is to send them $50,000, and Sacramento, CA, will get $2.00."

"That sounds like a scam."

"I know." Again I pause. This is getting good. "I kept that guy on the phone asking questions for almost 35 minutes."

"That is funny."

"I know, right? Keeping a sales person on the phone for a long time for something that you know you probably won't even buy."

"Exactly."

"I asked questions that didn't even apply to me."

"You are really funny."

"Thanks. I'm thinking about writing a book about telemarketers and my conversations with them."

"I'd read it."

"Hey, I bet I could put you in my book."

All I heard was a click.

About the author

Ray has been a funny guy for a while, but he suddenly decided to share his exploits with others, and we appreciate it. He can be reached via email: OnThePhoneWithRay@GMail.Com

Made in the USA
San Bernardino, CA
17 May 2020